This signed edition

has been specially bound by the publisher.

Rachel Macy Stafford

ONLY LOVE TODAY

OTHER BOOKS BY RACHEL MACY STAFFORD

Hands Free Mama

Hands Free Life

ONLY LOVE TODAY

REMINDERS to BREATHE MORE, STRESS LESS, and CHOOSE LOVE

Rachel Macy Stafford

New York Times Bestselling Author

ZONDERVAN®

ZONDERVAN

Only Love Today

Requests for information should be addressed to:
Zondervan, *3900 Sparks Dr. SE, Grand Rapids, Michigan 49546*

ISBN 978-0-310-35025-5 (signature edition)

ISBN 978-0-310-34949-5 (international trade edition)

ISBN 978-0-310-35029-3 (audio)

ISBN 978-0-310-34675-3 (ebook)

Library of Congress Cataloging-in-Publication Data

Names: Stafford, Rachel Macy, 1972-author.
Title: Only love today: reminders to breathe more, stress less, and choose love / Rachel Macy Stafford.
Description: Grand Rapids, Michigan: Zondervan, [2017]
Identifiers: LCCN 2016043333 | ISBN 9780310346746 (hardcover)
Subjects: LCSH: Christian life.
Classification: LCC BV4501.3 .S723 2017 | DDC 248.4—dc23 LC record available at https://lccn.loc.gov/2016043333

Cover design, hand lettering, and illustration: Kristi Smith, Juicebox Designs
Interior design: Kait Lamphere
Back cover image: Amy Paulson

First printing January 2017 / Printed in the United States of America

Dedicated to Delpha & Harry Macy
It was your example that inspired
my purpose, my prayer, and
eventually the words in this book.

Let me be love … because that's who
my parents raised me to be.

CONTENTS

INTRODUCTION

When your doctor tells you to stop at a drugstore on your way home and buy a blood pressure monitor, you do it.

Without giving it much thought, I chose the model that looked easy enough to administer. I planned to take my blood pressure a few times over the next several days to get an idea of what was going on with me.

When I got home, I immediately sat down at the kitchen table and started unpacking the box. I called out to Natalie, my twelve-year-old medical specialist-in-training, and asked her to help me.

"I know how to do that, Mama," she said, taking the cuff from me with capable hands and guiding my arm through the sleeve. "We learned this at emergency medicine camp last summer."

As she leaned over me in concern, my mind raced with worries ranging from dire to inconsequential. *What's wrong with me? Will I need blood pressure medication? Will Natalie and I make it to swim practice on time? What in the world am I going to make for dinner? Did I really wear one blue sock and one black sock to the doctor's office?*

Only love today, I silently repeated until the noise in my head quieted and I could be right where I needed to be—in *this* moment.

I felt the blood pressure cuff squeeze my upper arm and a few strands of Natalie's hair graze my skin. For the first time in a long time, I felt I was in good hands. That's when an unexpected blanket of peace settled over me, offering a crystal-clear perspective:

Those messy piles on the kitchen counter don't matter.

Those snug-fitting pants strewn on the floor of my closet don't either.

That opportunity I missed fifteen years ago and still think about today will need to go now.

That traffic I'll face taking Natalie to swim team practice won't faze me.

That person who always gives me the cold shoulder won't bother me today.

Even the nonstop rain sounds quite soothing as it beats down on the roof of my house for the ninth straight day.

As the cuff loosened and the numbers flashed, I decided I'd call my parents. I'd write a note to my husband, Scott, and place it on his pillow. I'd get that giant knot out of my younger daughter's hair softly, tenderly, and lovingly; Avery and I might even laugh about it. I'd go for a run in the rain with my music turned all the way up and cry if I felt like it. I'd write. I'd write beautiful words that would outlast me.

And that's exactly what I did with the hours of day that remained.

In that forty-five-second pause to check the status of my heart, I received the ultimate reprieve: the distractions fell away . . . the pressure subsided . . . the worries dissipated . . . the weight lifted. What mattered most came into clear focus.

Could this be the answer? I wondered. I'd always longed for a concrete way to keep my priorities straight—a way to put *love* at the top of the to-do list, above all else. But such an existence was not easy for a recovering perfectionist, reformed rusher, and professional multitasker. Questions, worries, and demands ran on a continuous loop through my head, causing me to choose productivity, distraction, and efficiency over feelings, connections, growth, and self-care far too often.

But in those sacred seconds when I could actually *feel* the blood pulsing through my veins, I was able to catch my breath and prioritize the meaning-*ful* over the meaning-*less*. Thus, heart readings became my daily practice. I sat motionless, relishing the squeeze on my arm and the flash of clarity, knowing I'd experience greater intentionality throughout the remainder of the day. In those peaceful moments at the kitchen table, *only love today* became more than a mantra to recite; it became a reset button for my misdirected soul.

"You don't need to do that anymore," Scott said a few months later as Natalie and I huddled together over the cuff like it was our job.

He was referring to what I'd learned at my doctor visit the day before: my elevated blood pressure had returned to normal. I was on a healthy path, and I no longer needed to monitor it daily.

"Yes. I do," I told my husband, feeling quite certain nothing would ever stop me from taking my blood pressure.

What Scott didn't know was that I'd taken an informal inventory of what had transpired since I purchased that cuff. I'd taken more walks . . . more naps . . . more risks. I'd given more second chances . . . more loving glances . . . more three-second pauses. I'd given away less of my most precious commodities, such as time, focus, and energy, so I'd have plenty for the people I loved. I stopped mindlessly scrolling and accepting requests out of guilt; I declined social gatherings that drained me; I reduced unnecessary commitments, time-wasting distractions, and interactions with toxic people. In other words, the cuff had empowered me to channel love into the most important areas of my life despite what the outside world was pressuring me to do. The daily blood pressure reading was my remedy for the ailments of too busy, too tired, too stressed, too hurried, and too distracted. In forty-five seconds, it cleared away the fog so I could seize what mattered most.

As I watched those numbers flash, I wished everyone could experience the illuminating power of the blood pressure cuff the way I had.

One day I realized they could.

I asked God to use me as a messenger, to use my hands, heart, and eyes to write short reflections that would breathe life into weary bones, cultivate hope in hopeless hearts, and point each day in a positive direction.

And he did. Right here in this book.

Only Love Today.

I considered making this a daily inspiration book, but I didn't want to add more pressure to our already overly scheduled lives. I know when I'm handed a book that requires daily interaction, I either read ahead or fall behind, leaving me feeling like I am always off track—that I am not reading it correctly. The beauty of this book is you cannot get off track. In fact, your heart is your guide in finding what you need from this book, when it is needed.

Organized by seasons of life, each section of readings will help you focus on the areas you need to breathe life into. As I was writing, three main themes emerged for each season, and you'll see those noted at the top of each entry. You might use those key words to guide you toward the reminders you need most. Perhaps you've lost your joy and yearn to find it again; perhaps you hope to repair broken connections; perhaps you want to love yourself "as is" and extend that same unconditional love to those who share your life; perhaps you want to pursue the passions of your heart but don't know where to start. Whatever is in need of love and attention, my prayer is that you find words here to recalibrate your life's direction, provide a positive path, and cultivate hope and healing along the way.

How you use this book is solely up to you. The readings can be used to help you begin the day with loving intentions. They can serve as nightly prayers to help you let go of the day's regrets, fall asleep with ease, and wake up renewed. They can be hourly lifelines to hold on to as you face periods of uncertainty, illness, loss, trauma, challenge, upheaval, or pain. On those days, you might find yourself consuming multiple readings in one sitting. On other days, you might let the book sit untouched on your bedside table. You'll know it's there if you need it, like a trusted friend. This book might even leave your possession for a bit if you offer it to a friend bookmarked with a sticky note on a certain page. Or perhaps you will run desperately to retrieve it when someone you love is hurt deeply or confused and you feel you have no words. In this book, may you find what you need.

This is not a *daily* inspiration book; it is a *moment-to-moment* encouragement book. Pick it up whenever your mind is distracted . . . your soul is frenzied . . . your heart is heavy . . . your connection is weak. May the words in this book remind you of the tools you already possess and the insights you already have to guide you back to what matters most, no matter what season of life you're in.

Only Love Today.

These three words have the power to resuscitate your heart . . . your home . . . your relationship . . . your dreams . . . and this precious God-given day before you.

Come. Sit with me. There's an empty place at my kitchen table where you can bravely reveal your struggles and scars. As you hear the words "Me too" whispered back through the pages of this book, take comfort in knowing you are not alone, there is hope, and you are in good hands.

Only Love Today—it's clarity when you are conflicted.

Only Love Today—it's unity when you are divided.

Only Love Today—it's relief when you are hurting.

Only Love Today—it might just be the reset button you've been looking for.

Let's see clearly together, my friend.

ONLY LOVE TODAY AFFIRMATION:

Today I will choose love. If I mistakenly choose distraction, perfection, or negativity over love, I will not wallow in regret. I will choose love next. I will choose love until it becomes my first response . . . my gut instinct . . . my natural reaction. I will choose love until it becomes who I am.

Let love start this day.
Let love end this day.
Let love transform the minutes in between.

Spring: Opening Up

Renewal, New Habits, and Growth

Today matters more than yesterday.
Who you are becoming matters more than who you were.

When Natalie became interested in making loose-leaf iced tea, it quickly became her passion. We'd seek out new flavors at rustic farmers' markets and fancy teashops. She'd hold out the canister and ask the vendor questions I did not understand. She'd pay with her babysitting money and carry her purchase securely with both hands. But it wasn't until we got home that I fully appreciated what was transpiring. As Natalie poured freshly boiled water over the tea leaves, I found myself awestruck by her sudden maturity and independence.

In an effort to help me ditch diet soda once and for all, Natalie would entice me with delicious flavor combinations. "Pomegranate peach," she'd say as she patiently allowed the tea to steep. "I think you'll like this one, Mama."

When the tea was chilled, she'd hold out a glass of the deep orange liquid, as if handing me a sunset made with her very own hands.

I felt like crying every single time.

One day it dawned on me why. The same place where Natalie made tea was precisely where I smashed a casserole dish in a moment of anger and overwhelm. And when I did, I scared that precious child, who happened to be rinsing off her dinner plate at the time.

This woman who is supposed to have it all together fell apart right in the very spot this child makes tea in hues of yellow, purple, and orange.

Each time my daughter handed me a glass and said, "Taste this one, Mama," I felt like I was being handed forgiveness, redemption, and the promise of a new dawn. I was reminded that even the best stumble sometimes. Even the one who holds up the world needs a reprieve. Even the most mindful need to evaluate their priorities every once in a while. I was reminded that even those who appear the most vibrant on the outside can be dying on the inside. I'd blink back tears as I recalled pieces of ceramic flying in every direction and how my daughter loved me in spite of it.

I look back on that unseasonably warm spring day and realize I was in a bad place. I was sleep-deprived. I was trying to meet work deadlines and fulfill end-of-the-school-year duties. I'd been in physical pain for months. I was worried about an infection I couldn't seem to shake. In this fragile state I made a mistake that could have hurt someone I love or myself.

That night I went to Natalie's room to ask for forgiveness. "I am so sorry," I said. "I did not handle the situation well. I think it's because I'm not taking good care of myself lately," I said. I was realizing and admitting this truth all at once.

My little budding orthopedic surgeon (who reads medical textbooks in her spare time "for fun") quickly came up with suggestions as if she'd been waiting to be asked. *More sleep, Mama. More fresh air. More water, Mama. Too much caffeine. More chilling out. Get your heart rate up when you exercise. And tea. Drink herbal tea instead of soda. I can make you some, Mama.*

I publicly declared then and there what I intended to do to get to a better place. I would give up soda and drink more water. I would add a little running into my daily walks; a mile or two of heart-pumping, sweaty exertion could do wonders. I would be more selective when it came to writing and speaking opportunities. I would get at least seven hours of sleep. I would go to a specialist and get to the bottom of a six-month-long bladder infection instead of continuing to take a multitude of antibiotics.

That is precisely what I did. I made changes. By the grace of God, it wasn't too late to get to a better, healthier place. I quickly began sleeping through the night. I could think more clearly. I could handle frustration better. I began advocating for my health, making it the top priority on my weekly agenda.

Change: it's possible. Failings: they're part of life. Growth: it's a gift. Whether you've lived many decades on this earth or just a few, it's not too late to evaluate the way you're living and make changes. It's not too late to be the person you want to be. Take it from me, a living, breathing example of a woman restored and renewed by small, daily efforts and the everlasting grace of God.

Natalie makes tea several times a week in the exact spot where things were broken but have managed to come back stronger than before. When she hands me that tall glass of forgiveness, I am given a reminder that brings relief to my parched soul—and now I offer it to you.

To you, the weary nurturer who begins each day feeling lost and overwhelmed . . .

to you, the hopeful artist praying for inspiration . . .

to you, the feisty survivor wondering what your pain level will be today . . .

to you, the broken-hearted believer searching for answers and hope . . .

to you, the silver-haired dreamer not quite ready to give up on the dream . . .

to you, the fearful protector facing what feels like a losing battle . . .

to you, the perpetual worrier wringing her hands over the state of things . . .

You are not finished. *Today matters more than yesterday. Who you are becoming matters more than who you were.* I offer the readings in the season ahead in the hope that they will be your tall glass of forgiveness, your undiscovered options, your promise of a new dawn. Each entry is a tangible lifeline toward positive change, renewal, and growth. Today offers one empty box in the calendar of life. Use it to do one good thing for your body, heart, mind, or soul despite its inconvenience at a time like this. Then do it again tomorrow, and the day after that, and the day after that. With God's grace, let us begin the hopeful restoration of our eager souls.

1

New Habits

One different element = a starting point to a better way of life

ONE DIFFERENT ELEMENT

If you could be more positive, would you?
If you could change your outlook, would you?
If you could speak in a more loving tone, would you?
If you could be more patient, would you?
If you could let go of the need to control, would you?
If you could start over, would you?

Sometimes when I am disgusted with myself and my negative ways, I remind myself of this:
That More Peaceful Person started with one calm reaction in the midst of chaos.

That More Positive Person started with one silver-lining comment in the midst of a downpour.

That More Attentive Person started with one question and a vow to listen, really listen, to the response.

That More Mindful Person started with five undistracted minutes on a sunlit porch.

That More Health-Conscious Person started with one mile and sixteen ounces of water.

That More Receptive Person started with an open hand and a "How would you do it?"

The improved version of yourself begins with one different element—a different reaction . . . a different word . . . a different routine . . . a different perspective . . . a different investment . . . a different choice.

If you could change the way this day is going, would you?

Try one different element. It might just be the start of a better way of life.

Today's Reminder

Today I will go public with my desired change by announcing a small, daily goal to a family member or someone else I trust. A public declaration might be something like this: I am making an effort to refrain from using the phone while I am driving. I may need your gentle reminders. Would you help me? *Or,* I am making an effort to put away my electronic devices during key connection times—such as mealtimes, bedtimes, greetings, and good-byes. Would you like to do this together? *Or,* I am making an effort to use a peaceful response in times of stress. Would you put your hand on your heart when I am hurting you with my words or tone as a reminder of my promise? *These small, daily actions of love, patience, and presence will soon become who I am, and they are how I will be remembered someday.*

2

Growth

Firsts can build confidence,
bring dreams closer,
and be the start of a new beginning and
better days to come.

FIRSTS

Maybe it's your first job interview.
Maybe it's your first day putting beloved people on the bus.
Maybe it's your first real attempt at living a better life.
Maybe it's your first day without someone you love.
Maybe it's your first day of putting on a pair of running shoes.
Maybe it's the first day you believe dreams really can come true.
Maybe it's your first day doing something you've never done before.
Maybe it's the first day you won't know anyone there.
Maybe it's the first day you need directions to get where you're going.
Maybe it's the first day you can find the strength.
Maybe it's the first day you've chosen to forgive.
Maybe it's the first day you find the time to do what you've been promising to do.
Maybe it's not *your* first, but the first for someone you love
or the first for someone standing next to you.
That may explain the nail biting, the stuttering, the grouchiness, the uncertainty.

Because firsts are hard.
Firsts are scary.
Firsts can be painful, intimidating, and stressful.
But with just the right amount of patience, compassion, and encouragement
for yourself
or someone you love
or that person standing next to you,
firsts can build confidence,
bring dreams closer,
and be the start of a new beginning and better days to come.

Today's Reminder

Stepping out of my comfort zone is not easy, but each time I do there is growth. Today I understand that fear and anxiety are normal reactions to new experiences. So in light of the new opportunities I face, I will practice a little extra kindness and a little more compassion than normal. I look forward to experiencing the growth that comes from stepping out of my comfort zone or taking a leap of faith.

3

Growth

By being softer you can hear more, learn more, feel more, and love more.

VOW TO SOFTEN

I've had enough of my hard edges.
I'm tired of straining my voice.

I'd like to loosen up and laugh a little more,
be positive rather than negative.

I'd like to feel the upward curve of my lips.
I'd like to surrender control of things over which I have
no control.
I'd like to let things unfold in their own time, in their
own way.
I'd like to participate joyfully in this fleeting life.

I'd like to be softer
toward him,
toward her,
toward myself.

Thus, this will be the year of my softening.
And this is my vow:

I vow to listen to opinions. I don't always have to be right.
I don't always have to agree or have the last word.

I vow to hand over the hairbrush, the pile of laundry, the
school project, the task before me.
"How would you do it?" I will ask.

I vow to step aside and respect a new approach.
Success might be difficult to see at first; I vow to keep
looking.

I vow to be more accepting of quirks and mannerisms.
I vow to be more accepting of tastes and styles unlike
my own.

I vow to remember he is in the process of becoming; she is in the process of finding her way.
And they are more apt to do it if I stop telling them how.

I vow to regard "weaknesses" as hidden strengths. Inner gifts can be nurtured when I stop plotting ways to alter, change, and "improve."

I vow to greet my family—and myself—with a loving smile, no matter what happened yesterday. Grudge-holding only hurts us all.

I vow to pause before correcting. I will take a moment to consider if the mistake even needs to be mentioned at all.

I vow to stop nitpicking until it bleeds.
I vow to demand less and inquire more.
I vow to listen,
consider,
and expand my thinking.

I vow to be a voice of encouragement in a demeaning world.
I vow to be a silver lining spotter in my family's little world.
I vow to be softer today than I was yesterday—a softer voice, a softer posture, a softer touch, a softer thought, a softer timetable.
I vow to be softer toward the imperfect human being inside me and the one beside me.
By being softer I can hear more, learn more, feel more, and love more.
At last I will fully see.
I will see his colors.
I will see her colors.

I will see my colors.
Perhaps for the very first time.
The colors might take my breath away,
bring me to tears,
or offer long-awaited peace.
I will soften in order to illuminate the colors of the soul.
I will soften so the human being within me and beside me can shine.

Today's Reminder

It is not always possible for me to choose love in the midst of challenging situations, but I can definitely try to soften—soften my voice, my touch, my opinion, and my timetable. Even a little softening goes a long way to bring peace to the situation. Today I will celebrate each time I soften when my first instinct is to harden.

4

New Habits

For the sake of your health, happiness, and beloved relationships,
choose to live the "alive" way.

Time Is on My Side

Time is on my side when I go to wake my sleeping loves, and I stop to watch their little chests rise and fall.
Time is on my side when I stop to give someone an airport good-bye even though we are not at the airport.

Time is on my side when I turn off the noise of the world
and tune in to the precious cargo riding in my backseat.
Time is on my side when I taste my food and feel thankful
for it.
Time is on my side when I express appreciation to someone
who's been good to me.
Time is on my side when I call an aging relative for a quick
check-in or a long "I love you."
Time is on my side when I turn up my favorite song and lose
myself in the lyrics.
Time is on my side when I finally sit down, and one of my
favorite people cuddles up against me.
Time is on my side when I take a long walk in nature and
listen for God's reassuring whispers among the trees.
The clock will tell me there's no time for this.
After all, this is not the most effective, productive, or
efficient way to live.
But the heart will tell me this is the *alive* way to live,
the Not-On-Autopilot way to live,
the Breathing, Feeling, Noticing way to live.
For the sake of my health, happiness, and beloved
relationships,
I want to live the *alive* way.
Today I will be looking for ways to walk with time on my side,
sheltering a few precious moments from the harsh, frenzied
blur of the world rushing past me.

Today's Reminder

I am going to do things a little differently today. Today the clock will not run my life. My heart will run my life. When there is love to be given, I will resist the impulse to decide if I have time, because I know there is always, always time for love.

5

Renewal

All the mistakes, failures, poor choices, all the things you wish you could do over are gone. Today stands before you with arms wide open. All you have to do is grasp it.

YOU HAVE TODAY

My child wandered into the kitchen, clutching her stuffed bunny in one hand, sucking the thumb of her other hand. As I buttered toast, I expected her to grasp my leg and rest her cheek against it. But today she offered something more. And although there was a time when I would have been too rushed, too distracted, or too impatient to see it, this time I didn't miss it.

I got it before one more email, one more text message, or one more *yes* to an unnecessary commitment stole another precious moment.

I got it before one more "In a minute" or one more "Once I get this finished" caused life to pass me by.

I got it before one more "When I lose five more pounds" or one more "What will people think?" prevented me from dancing, laughing, and truly living.

I got it before one more empty, shallow, meaningless distraction robbed me of the kind of glorious experience that makes life worth living.

And because I "got" it, I saw a chance to grasp what really matters.

Without hesitation I turned away from my burning toast, unmade school lunches, and unsigned homework folders. I turned away from distraction and turned toward what—or rather *who*—really matters. I opened my arms and scooped her up, just as I did when she was a baby.

As I held my child, I was struck by a revelation that seemed almost too good to be true:

I have today. Yesterday is gone. All the mistakes, failures, poor choices, all the things I wish I could do over, they are gone.

Today stands before me with arms wide open.

This hopeful truth is yours too.

You are never too far gone to come back.

You are never too tarnished to be made new.

You are never too broken to be made whole.

It's never too late to make changes.

It's never too late to begin again.

It's never too late to choose love.

By the grace of God, today stands before us with arms wide open.

All we have to do is grasp it.

Today's Reminder

Today I will be mindful of who and what I push away in the name of efficiency, productivity, and distractibility. I will pause before I decide I am "too busy" to meaningfully connect, converse, or create. At least once today, I will stop myself before I say no *to what really matters.*

6

Growth

Today I will ask myself: What would love do?
I will ask myself again and again and let love lead me forward.

WHAT WOULD LOVE DO?

What would love do? I ask myself as I look in the mirror and start picking myself apart. Love would look past the reflection and say, "Look how far I've come." Love would say, "I'm grateful for another day."

What would love do when my growing child comes down the stairs wearing an angry scowl? Love would open its arms and say, "Getting up is hard, I know." Love would hold its tongue. Love would give a little more time and a little extra grace.

What would love do when it's obvious my spouse forgot to do something important? Love would take a deep breath and then say, "It's okay. I forget things too." Love would see all the things he remembers and thank him for that.

What would love do when ugliness fills my News Feed, stands behind me grumbling in line, or cuts me off in traffic? Love would not join in. Love would negate it by being kind to the coworker with sad eyes or helping the neighbor with heavy burdens.

What would love do when finances, commitments, duties, and demands make it hard to breathe? Love would lower the bar. Love would let something go. Love would ban the phrase "I should," and say, "Good enough for today."

What would love do when hate-filled words and cliques build barriers that keep people out? Love would look for the lonely, excluded, and alienated. Love would reach out a hand and say, "Come as you are. There's a place for you here."

Today I want to look like love.
I want to sound like love.
I want to speak like love.
Too often I look like worry, impatience, and agitation.
I'd rather look like love.
Too often I sound like arrogance, selfishness, and greed.

I'd rather sound like love.

Too often I'm all about productivity, efficiency, and time management.

I'd rather be all about love.

It's not easy—choosing love takes time, effort, thought, patience, and self-control.

But the payoff is huge.

Choosing love for myself and for those in my path means

a better morning,

a brighter outlook,

a deeper connection,

a softer place to lay my head at night.

I can be anything today.

I'm going to be love.

How about you?

Today's Reminder

Today I will keep these powerful truths in the forefront of my mind: I can add to a hostile climate, or I can neutralize it; I can fuel a heated argument, or I can defuse it; I can damage a connection, or I can nurture it—all through my response. In a culture quick to judge, attack, and ridicule, I want to be quick to be kind. I want to be a representative for love. I want to be a living example of what love can do when it is chosen again and again. Not only are my family members watching, learning, and following my lead, but I have to live with myself. I'd like to end this day (and someday, my life) knowing I made my little part of the world a more loving place.

7

New Habits

Perhaps you've never known how happy
someone could be simply to see you.

CREATING A SUN DELAY

I remember the first time I started collecting hellos.

Instead of staring at the screen of my phone or reviewing my to-do list that day, I simply watched for my child to exit the school doors.

When she did, I had to fight back the tears.

I never knew that the minute she emerges from that building, her eyes search for me.

I never knew that when she spots me, her eyes melt into tiny slivers of joy that seem to merge with the corners of her mouth.

I never knew that she vigorously waves her tiny hand as if she is waving to Mickey Mouse himself.

I never knew how her backpack happily bounces up and down as if she is walking on air to meet me.

I never knew someone could be this happy simply to see me. But now I do. Thank you, God, now I do.

That was the day I discovered nothing on a screen or a list could compare to the sight of my beloved's face as she comes towards me.

That was the day I started collecting hellos.

Someday this sacred collection will soften the pain of the inevitable good-byes.

Today's Reminder

When I greet my loved ones with happiness, excitement, interest, and love, the message I am sending is: You are loved. *Today I've decided that showing my family I'm happy to see them is important to me. I vow to let go of my distractions long enough to create a* sun delay, *which means: no matter what I am in the middle of doing, no matter how inconvenient it is to look up, no matter how busy I think I am, when my loved ones walk into the room or return after a separation, my world is going to stop for a moment so love from me can shine in their eyes and hearts.*

8

New Habits

Noticers are the thriving blossoms in a
concrete world,
reminding us to stop and feel our beating
hearts every chance we can.

WHEN I STOPPED TRYING TO CHANGE YOU, YOU CHANGED ME

I would still be getting sick from sheer exhaustion and sleep deprivation.

I would still be making my way through mile-long to-do lists and neglecting the most important tasks of life, such as living and loving.

I would have missed the mama bird who tucked her nest in the corner of my porch.

I would have been in at least one fender bender (or much worse) because of my rushing and multitasking ways.

I would have given up on tangerines because they take too long to peel.

I would have missed a thousand conversations that just come when you sit still and wait for words.

I didn't miss any of them, thanks to my child.

Embracing my daughter's enjoy-the-journey approach to life

didn't just alter my actions and my behavior; it changed my perspective, transformed my thought processes, and loosened the tightly wound fiber of my inner being.

Although I am a work in progress and sometimes revert to my old ways, I'm always rewarded when I remember to stop trying to change her so that she can change me.

It happened the other day as I struggled to fall in line with her leisurely pace on a walk. As I felt myself becoming impatient, I reminded myself who I was with. I told myself it was not a time to rush; it was a time to listen and learn from the greatest life coach I've ever known.

About midway through our walk, my daughter said, "When my team runs laps after swim practice, my favorite part comes right after the *No Parking* sign. There's a crack in the concrete where plants grow. Can you believe that? Plants growing out of concrete! That is my favorite part of the run."

As I do multiple times a day, I closed my eyes and thanked God for this child who shows me the power of pausing—pausing to notice and pausing to love.

I can't help but consider what life would be like if I'd chosen to tell her slow was bad. Where would we be? The world would have two less graspers of life. Our hearts would be less fulfilled. I would not be the writer I am today. My life could have very well been cut short. Instead, I am blessed to experience the joys that used to elude me.

Thanks to my daughter, I don't miss them anymore.

So to the Noticers of the world and those who are blessed to raise them, I say this:

Thank you for being. You are an anomaly in this fast-paced world. We need you. We desperately need you . . .

to notice the birds and the bruises beneath the skin,
to notice the change of seasons and the one being left out,
to notice his name and remember to say it with love,

to notice the ripples on the water and the color of the sky after sunset,
to notice the barista who could use a kind word or two.
Thank you, Noticers, big and small.
You are the thriving blossoms in a concrete world,
reminding us to stop and feel our beating hearts every chance we get.

Today's Reminder

Today will be a day of noticing—noticing my own breath, noticing when I need to slow down, noticing when I need to step outside and look up at the sky. Today I will notice others—the sadness in her eyes; his nervous laugh; the short, irritable responses. Instead of turning away in impatience and annoyance, let me go towards them and express compassion, or simply say, "Me too." A day of noticing can mean a better day, a better me.

9

Growth

My responses are more than just words.
They represent
who I am,
who I want to be,
and how I will someday be remembered.

I AM MY RESPONSE

I am my response to my child's mismatched outfit and the crumpled report card at the bottom of her backpack.

I am my response to my spouse who returned from the store without toilet paper but remembered the tailgate snacks.
I am my response to my anxious parent who repeats the same worries and insists on giving me coupons I do not need.
I am my response to my coworker with sad eyes and frequent absences.
I am my response to my fifteen-minutes-late hairdresser with a sick child.
I am my response to my neighbor with the litany of problems and little family support.
I am my response to the irate driver who cut me off and made an obscene gesture in front of my children.
I am my response to the waitress who got my order wrong.
I am my response to myself when I forgot the one thing I most needed to do today.
I am my response to spilled coffee, rain-soaked shoes, and middle-of-the-night throw-up.
My responses are not perfect. They are not always ideal. I am human, after all.
But if I try to offer responses underlined with
grace,
understanding,
kindness,
empathy,
and care,
that is something.
That is something.
Because my responses are more than just words.
They represent
who I am,
who I want to be,
and how I will someday be remembered.
Today I will not respond perfectly, I know.

But if I strive to communicate with hints of kindness and
traces of love,
that will be something.
That will be something
that could mean more than words.

Today's Reminder

In challenging moments, kindness may not always be my first response. But when I do choose kindness, the issue resolves more quickly and peacefully. A compassionate response holds saving power—power to save a bond, save a line of communication, save a person's pride, save a moment, save a day, maybe even save a life. Today my responses, if underlined with a little kindness and love, could be someone's saving grace.

10

Renewal

Today is as good a day as any to begin again.

LET'S START OVER

Let's start over.
Let's choose to hold our tongues, swallow harsh words,
offer grace.
Let's choose to love "as is," because that human being
is pretty awesome if we take time to look past the
mistakes and imperfections.

Let's start over.
Let's choose to look up, look at, look in.

Let's choose to pay attention, because if we take time to truly see what's in front of us, we'll find the person standing there is pretty amazing.

Let's start over.
Let's choose to chill, pause, slow down.
Let's choose to set aside our own agenda, because if we take time to be available for hugs and kisses, we'll find that person we're hugging and kissing is pretty lovable.

Let's start over.
Let's choose to absorb, listen, and learn.
Let's choose to be all there, because if we take the time to really know what makes her laugh and what makes her dream, we'll find that human being is pretty incredible.

Let's start over.
Right now. Right here. Let's not wait another day.
Let's choose to accept, forgive, and understand.
Let's choose to live, love, learn, fall down, and get back up.

Because life—despite its challenges and daily disappointments—holds moments of joy, hope, comfort, and peace when we choose to start over and offer a second chance to others and ourselves.
Let's start over. Today is as good a day as any to begin again.

Today's Reminder

When I choose to hold on to guilt, regret, and anger, the negative impact reaches far beyond me. This day is too precious to ruin in such a careless way. Today I will offer my loved ones and myself the gift of starting over—starting over begins with the words, "I am sorry" to the people I love, and "I am human" to myself. This journey is not about what happened yesterday; it is about the choices I make today.

11

Growth

When you make the choice to grasp what
really matters,
things often turn out better than expected.

DIG IN

The other day my daughter Natalie found a recipe for yeast rolls in her cookbook for kids. She asked with eager eyes if she could make them.

"Right now?" I asked with trepidation.

For various shallow and meaningless reasons, "now" did not seem to be a good time. But just behind her, hanging prominently on the kitchen wall, was the "Hands Free" summer contract I'd created for moments just like this, moments when Drill Sergeant Rachel threatened to squelch any chance I had at grasping what mattered.

Although I wasn't inclined to say yes, I did. And although Natalie would have been perfectly capable of making the rolls by herself, I asked if I could help. I even pressed my hands inside the bowl next to hers to knead the gooey substance I was certain would resemble (and taste) like rocks when it came out of the oven.

In that hour making bread, we did some laughing, some talking, and some quiet self-reflecting side by side.

Eventually the rolls came out of the oven. They were not pretty; they were misshapen and heavy. But to my surprise, they tasted heavenly.

As I looked at that pan of rolls, and my daughter's flour-dusted nose, I was reminded of some words I wrote in a blog post called "My Secret Life."

"I'm certain of one thing," I wrote, "A Hands Free Life is not one that can be created when I'm holding tightly to distraction. I'm determined now, more than ever, to keep filling the pages of my beautifully flawed yet memorable and gratitude-filled life."

Despite the choices of the past, today we are presented with a blank page. A beautifully flawed, yet memorable and gratitude-filled life is at our fingertips. But we must dig in—dig in to the gooey, heavenly mess that is life.

When we make the choice to grasp what really matters, things often turn out better than expected.

May you find a moment today to open your hands, say yes, and dig in.

Today's Reminder

Today I will draft a Hands Free contract with a few personal and family goals for this season. It might include doing fun projects, outdoor excursions, exercising, cooking, or just sitting down and relaxing more. It might include reading enlightening books or playing more games as a family, getting rid of excess and giving unneeded things to charity, or helping people or animals in need. I will talk to my family (or friends) about these goals and invite them to join me. I believe saying yes to more real-life experiences this season will benefit us all in countless ways.

12

New Habits

Why wait for the moment when you're
hoping and praying for a sign of life to
say the important things?
Why not make it an everyday occurrence
to give a sign of love?

A SIGN OF LOVE

My mom worked long hours when my sister and I were in middle and high school. We had many responsibilities at home, but my mom always took time to reinforce our efforts with randomly placed little notes. Even though she left very early, and sometimes didn't get home until very late, somehow she managed to leave us tangible reminders of her love and appreciation.

I believe it was the memories of my mother's notes that prompted me to start leaving notes for my daughters. To my amazement, my daughter Avery brought the powerful gesture full circle by writing notes back to me.

A few days after I'd discovered Avery's notes, I read a moving account of a Norwegian teenager who sent text messages to her mother while she hid from a mass shooter for over ninety minutes.

At the beginning of the ordeal, the girl's mother had asked her child to send "a sign of life" every five minutes.

So every five minutes a text came through. Some of the messages were frantic and scared; other times there were just three hope-filled words: "I'm still alive."

The daughter even had a moment to tell her mother, "I love you even though I yell at you sometimes."

These exchanges lasted until, finally, the mother was able to see on the news that the shooter had been captured. With great joy and relief, she texted her daughter: "They got him!"

This compelling story reminded me of something I too often forget. Why wait until I'm going to be separated from my loved ones to give them tangible signs of love? Why wait to tell the precious people in my life how much they mean to me? Why wait for the moment when I'm hoping and praying for a sign of life to say the important things? Why not make it an everyday occurrence to give a sign of love?

It's no more than a card on a bed, a sticky note on a mirror, a little message tucked inside a lunch box.

I often think about that brave mother who kept her wits about her as she agonized over the fate of her beloved daughter. I often think about their reunion and how life must have looked different from that point on. I can only imagine how many signs of love that mother will bestow on her daughter in the precious God-given days to come.

Today's Reminder

Today I will give a tangible sign of love to someone dear to me. A meaningful message can be written or spoken using one of these gratitude starters:

I'll never forget when you . . .

I appreciate how you . . .

I'm sorry that sometimes I . . .

What I love most about you is . . .

I have you to thank for . . .

Five words to describe you are . . .

Our family wouldn't be the same without your . . .

13

New Habits

When love speaks, we are all better heard.
When love looks, we are all better seen.

If It's Love

If it's love, those tears are a sign of distress, not an act of defiance.

If it's love, her bold fashion statement is something to be celebrated, not criticized.

If it's love, his mistakes are evidence of trying and learning, not simply messes to clean up.

If it's love, her slow pace is a reflection of her "stop and smell the roses" approach to life, not a time waster.

If it's love, his early morning wake-ups are something he'll outgrow, not a plot to exhaust us.

If it's love, her poor choice is a chance to respond thoughtfully, not give a knee-jerk reaction.

If it's love, our voice has a little more calm; our eyes have a little more perspective; our hands have a little more gentleness.

We won't always choose love. We are human, after all.

But when we choose love over anger, hurry, condemnation, shame, and sarcasm, there is space for goodness to enter the conversation.

When love speaks, we are all better heard.

When love looks, we are all better seen.

Let us look and speak love today. As much as we possibly can, let us allow goodness in.

Today's Reminder

In the busyness of life, it's easy to fall into the habit of saying my loved one's name as if it's just a word or a way to get his or her attention. Before I address my loved one today, I will take a moment to remember the time, thought, and care that went into choosing the name of this precious person, and then I'll say it with genuine love. This one simple action holds the power to bring love into the conversation.

14

Renewal

When we push away what is urgent, we are
able to see what is necessary.
Then we can hold it lovingly with both hands.

See What Is Necessary

I was once a professional putter-offer, meaning I consistently put off the best moments of life in order to attend to the urgent demands of life.

Too busy to laugh and play.

Too busy to just sit and talk.

Too busy to think.

Too busy to breathe.

In that delay of living well came a pretty unpleasant side effect—one I could not hide. In that delay of living well, the worst side of me came out.

All I have to do to remember how bad it got is to look at a particular picture of my family fishing in the mountains of Georgia. I was the one in the background—miserable, distracted, and disconnected. While they happily fished and talked, I faded away, consumed by a list of things I thought mattered greatly at the time. Now I cannot even remember what was so urgent.

I do remember talking my family into leaving that little vacation early. We left our dusty but cozy cabin in the mountains because my external demands and the approval of others were more important than my inner needs and inner circle.

I told only one person that painful truth, and not until years after it happened. I'll never forget how my friend touched my arm gently and said, "I am glad you don't shorten your vacations anymore."

When you start to shorten your vacations, you shorten your life. And by "vacation" I don't mean cabins, hotels, or beaches. I mean reconnection, restoration, and rejuvenation. Vacation can happen in your own home, simply by turning off the world and turning toward your inner needs and inner circle.

When you take away what is urgent, you find what is necessary.

Let me tell you what I've found is necessary in case your soul is feeling frenzied today:

It is necessary to nurture your body.
It is necessary to nurture your mind.
It is necessary to nurture your soul.
It is necessary to nurture your romantic relationship.
It is necessary to nurture your parent-child bonds.
It is necessary to nurture your faith, your spiritual self, and your passions.

If you are like me, and sometimes need to be reminded of what is *not* necessary, here's some reality:

It is not necessary to respond to all the emails in the inbox.
It is not necessary to text back immediately.

It is not necessary to have social media apps at your fingertips or electronic notifications turned on.
It is not necessary to check your phone first thing in the morning or right before bed.
It is not necessary to feel guilty when you say no.
It is not necessary to please others at the expense of your family or your health.
It is not necessary to do tasks at a proficiency level of 100 percent.
It is not necessary to clean up the kitchen before sitting down.
It is not necessary to take homemade baked goods to the party—store-bought taste good too.
It is not necessary to wash your hair to go out—a hat works just fine.
It is not necessary to deprive yourself of sleep in order to accomplish everything.
It is not necessary to deprive yourself of *living life* in order to accomplish everything.

We cannot change the lost moments when we were emotionally absent. But we can do something about the present moments we feel ourselves fading from today. We can push away what is urgent so we can see what is necessary. Then we can hold what is necessary lovingly with both hands.

Today's Reminder

Today feels like a good day for this collection of life-saving truths: Even losing myself in good works is still losing myself. Even the one who handles everything must rest and restore. Even the most mindful need to evaluate their priorities every once in a while. Even the best stumble sometimes. In these moments of human vulnerability, my loved ones have a chance to lift, love, and carry the one who often lifts, loves, and carries them.

15

RENEWAL

The more you choose by heart, the more
you choose what matters to you,
not what matters to the rest of the world.

THREE QUESTIONS TO LIVE BY HEART

I asked my distracted, overcommitted, stressed-out self three questions to help me start investing in what mattered most:

Does the amount of time and attention I currently offer my family and my health convey that they are top priorities in my life? The answer was no.

Does my current schedule allow time to be fully present with my loved ones or nurture my well-being? The answer was no.

Do I have any extracurricular commitments or time-wasting distractions I could eliminate in order to invest a few minutes in my relationships and self-care? The answer was yes. *Yes.* Oh yes, there was hope.

That is when I realized:

I cannot control all the circumstances of my life, but I can control some.

I cannot let go of all my extracurricular commitments, but I can let go of some.

I cannot say no to every outside request asked of me, but I can say no to some.

I cannot rid myself of all modern-day distractions, but I can designate small amounts of time each day to turn off the world and be available to the people who matter most (including me).

And that's exactly what I did.

Every time I turned off the world and turned toward my family and my well-being, my heart felt I was right where I was supposed to be.

The more I chose by heart, the more I chose what mattered to me, not what mattered to the rest of the world.

With the help of these three questions, I've gotten closer to the life I want to live—a life of meaning, knowing my people, caring for myself, and engaging in things that could become my legacy when I'm gone.

Today's Reminder

Today I am going to create a morning habit that will lead to more time, more patience, and more living in my day. I will not begin my day by reaching for the phone. When I pick up the phone to start my day, I get further from the life I want to live. Information, messages, and requests take me away from what matters to me *and shifts it to what matters to everyone else. Instead, when I rise, I will reach for faith, human connection, or self-care. Mornings can be about not missing my digital connections or they can be about not missing my soul connections. I choose the latter. I refuse to miss my life.*

16

New Habits

There is peace in knowing you spent today living
your happily ever after
instead of tacking it to the bottom of the to-do list
where it will never be touched.

UNDISTRACTED LOVE

It is possible to become quite skilled at putting off your happily ever after.

Once I get this work done . . .

Once this project is finished . . .

After I make these calls . . .

In just a minute . . .

Once the project is complete, the minute has passed, and the calls have been made, something else always comes up. At least that's how it was for me; my "one more thing" had no end.

Then troubling things start to happen. You drive into the intersection before it's your turn because you're looking at a screen. You scream at the ones you love because you're stretched too thin. You wake up feeling irritable and unhappy, the same way you went to bed. Finally, one sad day, someone you love dearly leaves this earth far too soon. That's when it hits you: your happily ever after is slipping right through your busy little fingers. You begin to understand the fragility of life, the true gift of today.

So you begin looking straight into the eyes of the ones you love.

You begin listening to their silly, tender words so you don't miss a thing.

You begin saying yes to familiar faces and opportunities to cuddle.

You turn off the world and tune in to what matters.

That's when you see it. Feel it. Believe in it.

Undistracted love.

It's living your happily ever after now. In little, loving ways. Every. Single. Day.

Undistracted love.

It's the kind of love that gets you through the hard times and makes the good times even sweeter.

It's the kind of love you can stand on.

It's the kind of love that holds you up.

It's the kind of love that leaves you with no regrets, even when you're faced with the unexpected and unplanned.

Regardless of what tomorrow holds, there is peace knowing you spent today living your happily ever after instead of tacking it to the bottom of the to-do list where it will never be touched.

Next time you're in the presence of someone you love, instead of reaching for distraction, think of these words:

She's right there; hold her.
He's right there; talk to him.
She's right there; ask about her day.
He's right there; look into his eyes.
She's right there; kiss her.
He's right there; listen to him.
She's right there; tell her she's beautiful.
He's right there; embrace him.
He's *right there.*
She's *right there.*

Love each other today in such a way that you couldn't possibly love each other more.

Today *is* your happily ever after—don't delay it one more day.

Today's Reminder

Today I will think of three things I love about my spouse or someone else I care for deeply. I will tell that person those things and request we schedule daily and/or weekly undistracted and uninterrupted time with each other. I vow to nurture my relationship. What we nurture thrives, and I want this bond to flourish and strengthen.

17

GROWTH

Don't wait to live the life you've been
yearning to live.
There's joy to be found, and it starts today
with a single step.

DON'T WAIT

It was the "year of the hill" at our house. My children slid down the hill for the first time in February 2010 and didn't let up for twelve months.

The number of times the sisters went down the hill must be in the hundreds, which led me to believe that each trip down was a unique experience. They never knew where that flat piece of cardboard would take them. They never quite knew where they'd end up.

When I think about their favorite activity of 2010, I have one predominant thought: *thank goodness they didn't wait for snow to slide down that hill.*

Because they never would have gone down.

It never snowed once in our mild climate, but that did not stop my two girls from sledding. This powerful truth makes me think about the mistake many of us adults make when we put off our dreams until conditions are "right." The snowless hill of joy makes me think about the way we too often place time limitations on pursuing passion and fulfillment.

When I am not so busy . . .

When I lose fifteen pounds . . .

When I have more time . . .

When I get my personal issues sorted out . . .

When things slow down at work . . .

Suddenly we find another year has gone by, and we still haven't started doing what our heart longs to do.

It doesn't have to be that way. Who cares if conditions aren't perfect? There's a hill to be conquered and joy to be found. I say, don't wait.

Don't wait to fill that notebook. *There's a story to be written. And it starts with one word.*

Don't wait to put on those running shoes. *There's an open pathway to a healthier life, and it starts with one mile.*

Don't wait to shed that heavy cloak of self-deprecation. *There's a beautiful you waiting to emerge, and it starts with "I am worthy."*

Don't wait to nurture a precious relationship. *There's a human being waiting to be loved, and it starts with "I'm here now."*

Don't wait to simplify your life. *There's excess needing to be purged, and it starts with the word* no.

Don't wait to take a risk. *There's a leap of faith to take, and it starts with the word* yes.

Don't wait to live the life you've been yearning to live. *There's joy to be found, and it starts today with a single step.*

Today's Reminder

Today I will write down as many personal dreams as I can think of in five minutes. There is nothing too outlandish or ridiculous for my dream list. Later today I will go back and circle one dream on the list to put into action. I will write down one small first step to take and set a deadline. I will keep setting and accomplishing small steps toward my dream until it is no longer just a dream.

18

RENEWAL

No matter how tired, stressed, or distracted
I am going into her room,
I come out feeling renewed.

TALK TIME

"I like the way you take your time putting me to bed," my daughter Natalie said.

I looked over my shoulder, thinking she couldn't be talking to me. "Take your time" and my name didn't belong in the same sentence—at least they didn't used to.

For years I was always in a hurry. Life was one big race. There was always something needing to be done. Idle time was wasted time. Important things were what could be checked off a list, written on a sticky note, or tapped into a device with lightning-fast fingers.

Such an exhausting pace could not be maintained. It was at my daughter's bedtime that I'd finally slow down.

Just be here, I thought to myself one night. *Just be right where I am now*, I vowed as I snuggled in close. *Don't think about the dishes piled in the sink, or the messages in the inbox, or the trash needing to go curbside, or the ache in your hip in need of an ice pack. Just think about the precious girl in need of a little time with her mom.*

So I focused on her sun-kissed hair falling across her cheek, the way her pillow smelled like Suave shampoo, and the way my breath steadied in time with hers.

When Natalie noticed I wasn't in a hurry to leave, she talked. Then I talked. Ten minutes or twelve minutes passed—I stopped watching the clock.

Over time, those ten or twelve minutes at bedtime have become the most important minutes of the day.

It is softness in the glow of a night-light. It is hushed whispers and muffled giggles. It is blankets and warmth. It is human connection in its purest form.
It is where she voices the dream of being an orthopedic surgeon who volunteers with homeless animals on the weekend.
It is where she inquires about the colors of my wedding bouquet and the look on her daddy's face as I walked down the aisle.
It is where she told me she wanted to live in my house forever—would that be all right?
It is where I found out she was being bullied.
It is where I found out she'd made a serious mistake but trusted me with it.
It is where I find tenderness in her sometimes-tough exterior.
It is where I hear her darkest fears and heartfelt prayers.
It is where time stands still.

It might just look like a bed with a floral comforter containing a sleepy girl who loves to have Talk Time, but to me it is perfect peace.

No matter how tired, stressed, or distracted I am going into her room, I come out feeling renewed. It costs me ten minutes, but the payoff is huge. I get to hear things no one else gets to hear. Something tells me this is one daily investment I will never regret.

A little shared time and undivided presence allows me to see into my child's heart.

That's worth slowing down for.

Today's Reminder

Today I will make conditions right for listening to my loved ones. I will push aside distractions and stop doing anything else when they are speaking. I will be still and look into their eyes. I will preface the moment with, "I have ten minutes, and they are all yours." I will decide there is nothing more important than hearing their words. I will express gratitude for that period of time as it begins. I will acknowledge that these particular moments will never come again, and I will savor them.

19

Growth

What is most important in life cannot be
measured; but instead felt through
the hands,
heart, and soul of each life we touch.

WHAT CANNOT BE MEASURED

Get off the scale. It cannot measure the depths of your heart.

Put down the measuring stick. It is not long enough to assess your worth.

Ignore the score. It does not show your true potential.

Don't get hung up on the salary. It doesn't even come close to showing your value.

Ban the mirror. It cannot reflect how much you are loved.

Ignore the critic. It has no idea how far you've come.

Instead, look for evidence of a day well lived:

I made someone smile. I gave a tender kiss. I hugged and

wasn't the first to let go. I encouraged. I laughed. I believed. I lifted. I kneeled. I forgave. I lived. I loved.

What is most important in life cannot be measured; but instead felt through the hands, heart, and soul of each life we touch.

Today's Reminder

Life's most important achievements are not documented, measured, or checked off; they are felt in the heart. By putting so much focus on accomplishing things, *I am missing the best parts of life. It's time to stop losing myself in numbers and measurements. It's time to live freely and fiercely, just as I am. Time doesn't wait while I futilely try to "do it all." Time doesn't wait while I compare myself to this person or that person. Therefore, I choose to stop wasting precious time. Today I stop looking at the things I am not and start looking at all the things I am.*

20

New Habits

Allowing oneself to simply be in the moment at hand is a rare and beautiful gift.

WISHING AWAY TIME

I vividly remember the day I stopped wishing away time.

My four-year-old daughter had just picked a dandelion and was studying it intently.

"If you could go anywhere in the world right now, where would you go?" I asked, curious what she would say. I expected her response to involve seashells, cotton candy, grandparents, or *Toy Story* characters. But what she said left me speechless and a bit enamored.

"Picking dandelions with you," she replied without a moment's hesitation.

Out of any place in the world she could dream of being, my child chose to be right where she was in that very moment.

As my eyes filled with tears, I could recall too many unsettling lines that had come from my lips . . .

"I can't wait for school to start."

"I wish the warmer weather would finally get here."

"When is it going to be Friday? This week is killing me."

"Once I get through this busy month, we'll do something fun as a family."

"I look forward to the day she stops sucking her thumb."

To put it bluntly, I wished time away.

In this fast-paced, task-driven world, slowing down takes deliberate effort. Allowing myself to simply *be* in the moment at hand is a rare and beautiful gift.

How easily I forget there is no guarantee tomorrow will even come, or that tomorrow will be as wonderful as today.

Today I have my health, my happiness, and my security. But there may come a day when I won't. Thanks to the wisdom of a child, and the beauty of a dandelion, things are different now. Instead of wishing time away, I find myself praying time will stand still so I can savor the present just a little more.

Today's Reminder

Today I will take a moment to reflect on what I'd do if I had one month to live. How would that change my agenda? How would that change my perspective on the day's challenges or my family members' annoying habits? Today I will savor time in that morning wake-up, in that good-bye hug, in that dinnertime fellowship. I will remember my loved ones are constantly growing and changing, and things may be different tomorrow.

21

NEW HABITS

I just want to celebrate you as you are instead of waiting for you to become what the world expects you to be.

YOUR NUMBER ONE FAN

Each day I take time to say, "Did you get your homework? Did you brush your teeth? Don't forget your lunch money."

But do I take time to say the words you need to hear? "You matter. You're important. I love being with you. I love you for who you are."

Each day I take time to observe your grades, swim strokes, and table manners.

But do I take time to observe the joy on your face when you run through the grass or the way your eyes crinkle up when you laugh?

Each day I take time to know your schedule, where you need to be, and what supplies you need to have.

But do I take time to know you? To know what brings you peace? What makes you scared? What makes you feel safe? What makes you laugh 'til you cry?

Amid the rush, the pressures, and challenges of daily life, I tend to forget what is most important.

Honestly, when it comes right down to it, only a few things really matter.

I just want to hear you laugh.

I don't care about perfect pitch.

I just want to see you smile.
I don't care about golden trophies that shine.
I just want to give you a soft place to land.
I don't care about what place you come in.
I just want you to be comfortable in your skin.
I don't care about the blemish on your nose or the size of your jeans.
I just want to love you today, as you are.
I don't care about what the world expects you to be.

Sometimes I get off track. I let society tell me that achievements, awards, scores, and outer beauty are what matter most.

But those things are very, very far from what matters most to me. Your heart, your spirit, your spunk, and your inner light are what matter to me.

So today, as your number one fan, I will be listening and watching.

I just want to see you smile.
I just want to hear you laugh.
I just want to watch you shine.
I just want to celebrate you as you are
instead of waiting for you to become what the world expects you to be.

Today's Reminder

It's easy to fall into the trap of barking orders—to sound like a surly manager rather than a loving human being. Direction, guidance, and reminders are necessary at times, but they don't need to be spoken like a drill sergeant would. Today I will strive to be less of a dictator and more of a guiding, supportive, loving presence. I will nurture the people in my life, not manage them. Today I will offer my best to those who love me at my worst.

22

RENEWAL

Do less—you're missing more than life.
Be more—you've got so much to live for.

MISSING MORE THAN LIFE

It happens when I hear my husband laughing hysterically with my children in the next room.

It happens when I hear my younger daughter singing at the top of her lungs from her bedroom.

It happens when I hear my older daughter gathering baking pans and hoisting herself up on the counter to get a cookbook.

It happens when I hear my seventy-five-year-old mom say her back is stiff, so she's going to walk around the block.

These sounds cause me to surface from beneath the waves of my daily distractions and ask, "What am I missing right now?"

The answer?

I'm missing life; I'm missing the parts of life that really matter. This powerful truth causes me to make better choices with my time, energy, and focus.

It wasn't always this way. I used to tell myself, "I'll join them in a minute." But then a minute would become an hour, a day, a year; that momentary delay would often become one tragically long period of missed opportunities to simply *be* with the ones I love.

That's all they really wanted—for me to just be there—not doing, planning, shuttling, entertaining, or directing, but to just *be there.* My daughter Avery told me so one day at her sister's swim meet. I'd left my giant stack of to-do's at home, and for once my lap was free. Avery sat on it until my legs grew numb. I'll never forget how she looked up at me and whispered, "This is the kind of mom I always wanted."

By "this" I knew exactly what she meant.

Present.

Attentive.

Still.

Available.

Available.

Completely available to love her.

So the next time you get the feeling you'd like to slow down and enjoy a moment, maybe these words will inspire you:

Do less—you're missing more than life.

Be more—you've got so much to live for.

Today's Reminder

Today I will schedule time to pause—to stop, sit, be still, and simply be. I will say to myself: "This do-nothing moment is my breathing room. It's fuel for my soul." If my loved ones congregate around me while I pause, I will take it as an opportunity to love them. If they don't, I will take it as an opportunity to connect to my own heart and soul.

23

Renewal

As long as you are breathing, it's not too late to be the person you hope to be.

NOT TOO LATE

My first step to a less distracted life started with ten minutes. Ten minutes of pushing aside the phone, the computer, the to-do list . . . the regret, the resentment, the impatience . . . the guilt, the pressure, the doubt. I pushed them all away so I could be fully available *to love* and *be loved.*

Ten minutes. That is where I started.

So when someone asks me, "Is there hope for my distracted, hurried, perfectionistic ways?"

I say, "Start with ten minutes. No matter what happened yesterday, you can start right now."

You may have a mile-long list of mistakes and failures.

You may have yelled at your loved ones just a few minutes ago.

You may feel undeserving of another chance.

You may believe you cannot change.

I know. I remember.

But in that initial ten minutes of loving connection I had with my child, I experienced a healing peace I hadn't felt in years, maybe even decades. That is when I realized life was meant to be lived.

Not managed.

Not controlled.

Not screamed.

Not stressed.

Not strangled.

Not guilt-ridden.

Not regretted.

Not wasted by thinking it's too late to turn things around.

As long as you are breathing, it's not too late to try.

Believe one small step can make a difference.

Believe ten minutes of open hands and attentive eyes can bring healing love and meaningful connection back to your life.

Believe your life is meant to be lived, enjoyed, even celebrated, regardless of what happened yesterday.

If you are having a hard time believing, offer a few minutes to someone you love. Watch what happens when you offer yourself. Messy, scarred, or broken, it doesn't matter. By offering to *give* love, you are offering yourself a chance to *be* loved.

Be loved.

If you have ten minutes and a willing heart, it might just be enough to make a believer out of you. As long as you are breathing, it's never too late to try.

Today's Reminder

Right now, I will set a meaningful intention for the day ahead. I will ask myself what I want to get out of it. If a daily intention seems too overwhelming, I will set my intentions for a ten-minute period within today. In a ten-minute period protected from distraction and pressure, a loving connection can happen, a memory can be made, and a path can be paved for a more positive day ahead.

24

Renewal

The most meaningful life experiences don't
happen in the "when";
they happen in the "now."

WHEN ALL IS RIGHT WITH THE WORLD

Do you ever have a moment when all is right with the world? A private tea party for two.

A tender conversation between a girl and her dog.
A couch full of all the people you love, happily squished against you.
In that moment, all is right with the world.
No fighting, no whining, no chaos—just peace.
No deadlines, no distractions, no demands—just freedom.
No yesterday, no tomorrow, no long-term agenda—just now.
No failings, no criticism, no guilt—just love.
In that moment, all is right with the world.

These moments are brief. They are rare. They can be easily missed. Believe me, I know. I'm trying not to let them pass me by anymore.

This is how:

Pause in the busyness of your day—even a moment or two will do. For that moment, pay attention. Notice. Listen. Stop. Breathe.

There's a good chance you'll catch a moment when all is right in your perfectly imperfect, gloriously messy, happily chaotic little world.

Peace, love, freedom, and joy, right there at your fingertips.

The most meaningful life experiences don't happen in the "when"; they happen in the "now."

It is the sacred pauses within everyday life that heal our frenzied souls.

Let us pause and live today.

Today's Reminder

Although nothing may feel right in my world at the current moment, I can pause and acknowledge these truths: I don't have to know how it's all going to work out. I don't have to know where it begins and ends. I just need to know there is goodness in the middle of this mess. I will pause to notice and breathe. There's something divinely magical about breathing, trusting, and surrendering in moments of doubt that calms my anxieties and reveals the goodness found in today.

25

New Habits

Bring the Love.
Give the Love.
Embrace the Love.
Be the Love.

WHEN LOVE GETS LOST

I vividly remember sitting in my car one day, several years ago, waiting for my children to burst through the school doors. That entire day I'd felt unsettled, as if something was missing, but I couldn't put my finger on it.

When my children ran toward the car, I unexpectedly got out and held out my arms. My daughter Avery collapsed into them as if she'd been waiting all day for me to offer her a hug. As I held her, I realized what I'd been missing. Each morning our good-bye hug and kiss were getting lost in the hunt for shoes, eyeglasses, and homework.

That night I admitted to Avery that I didn't want to forget to share a loving good-bye each day. My ukulele-playing child went right to work creating a reminder sign for the door that read: "XOXO Before You Go."

The next morning, as I grabbed the car keys in my usual rush, Avery called out, "XOXO Before You Go!" as she pointed to the sign.

I remember how Natalie rolled her eyes as if to say she was too mature for such nonsense, but when I hugged her, she relaxed into me and inhaled my scent. She'd been missing the love too. I think it happens to all of us at one time or another.

If you find yourself a little lost, a little empty, or a bit unsettled, might I suggest *bringing the love*?

To the morning wake-up . . .

to the hurried send-off . . .

to the reunion after a separation . . .

to the darkened hours at bedtime.

These moments within our daily routine have the potential to bring meaning and connection to the sacred spaces of our lives—spaces that can be so easily filled with duties, activities, impatience, and stuff that doesn't really matter in the grand scheme of things.

When the love gets lost, it can leave a gaping hole. Thankfully, it's easily filled. With a little presence, some intention, perhaps a sign on the door and a kiss on the cheek, we can bring the love back.

Today, let's do this:

Bring the Love.
Give the Love.
Embrace the Love.
Be the Love.
Let Love fill the spaces that have yearned for its return.

Today's Reminder

Before I part ways with my beloved people today, I will give them "airport good-byes," meaning I will hold them for at least ten seconds, hug them tightly, inhale their scents, say "I love you," no matter what happened in the frustrating or hurried minutes before that good-bye. Today, giving airport good-byes becomes my daily ritual. Those ten seconds will be among the most sacred moments of my day.

26

Growth

I will choose love until it becomes my first response, my gut instinct, my natural reaction.
I will choose love until it becomes who I am.

WHY CHOOSE LOVE?

Tackle an extra hour of paperwork, or love?
I choose love.
I will be more productive after taking a much-needed break.

Scream at the driver who just cut me off, or love?
I choose love.
It will be better for my blood pressure as well as the ears in the backseat.

Read a text message at the stoplight, or love?
I choose love.
It could save my life, save my loved ones' lives, and spare me from taking a life.

Hold a grudge, or love?
I choose love.
Let resentment be someone else's lifelong companion.

Say, "I'm too busy to play," or love?
I choose love.
Seeing her smile as she sets up the game board fills me with a sense of peace I can't find in a constant stream of busyness.

Get in the last word, or love?
I choose love.
Our words will be better heard when we both cool down.

Rant about the spilled milk, or love?
I choose love.
Spills can be cleaned up; broken hearts are harder to mend.

Post a picture of this moment to social media, or love?
I choose love.
I will remember it more vividly if I capture this moment solely with my eyes.

Complain about the way she's dressed, or love?
I choose love.
I will encourage her to shine her unique light and be herself by loving her just as she is.

Berate myself for messing up, or love?
I choose love.
Accepting my humanness offers my precious ones the freedom to be human too.

Today I will choose love.
Tomorrow I will choose love.
The day after that, I will choose love.
If I mistakenly choose distraction, perfection, or negativity over love, I will not wallow in regret. I will choose love next.
I will choose love until it becomes my first response, my gut instinct, my natural reaction.
I will choose love until it becomes who I am.

Today's Reminder

Let me consider the possibilities for a moment: What might result if love becomes my default choice today? What opportunities might open up? What connections might be repaired? What moments might I capture that otherwise might be missed? Who might I start becoming? Today I have the chance to make grand possibilities come to life. I will choose love as much as I humanly can.

27

Renewal

Today I will save some goodness for those who save me.

SAVE SOME GOODNESS

I have only so much patience.
I have only so much energy.
I have only so much focus.
I have only so much strength.
I am human, after all.
Instead of giving it all away,
Instead of spending 'til it's gone,
Instead of using up my best,
I will save.
Save a little for the one who cuddles up.
Save a little for the one who lifts when I'm down.
Save a little for the one who helps me grow.
I have only so much enthusiasm.
I have only so much serenity.
I have only so much grace.

I am human, after all.
Let me save a little for the one who greets me with hugs.
Let me save a little for the one who forgives my failings.
Let me save a little for the one who wipes away my tears.
Today let me save some goodness for those who save me.

Today's Reminder

Whether it's helping my child get a knot out of her shoelace, conversing with my spouse, or walking beside my aging parent, I will tell myself, "Be where you are now," rather than constantly thinking ahead to what's next on my agenda or considering what else I should be doing. Giving myself permission to "be where I am now," whether it's two minutes or twenty, offers me the chance to love and be loved, and that is much more fulfilling than squandering my most priceless resources and coming up empty.

28

Growth

Learn when to wait a moment and when to seize *a moment*
so happiness has the time and space to come back in.

WHEN TO WAIT AND WHEN TO SEIZE

Wait for the perfect wave,
but don't wait for a vacation to spend time with the people you love.

Wait for your little straggler to catch up,
but don't wait for the scale to tell you when to jump into the pool.

Wait for the marshmallow to turn the perfect shade of brown,
but don't wait for a bigger table to invite friends over to eat.

Wait for your loved one to get his words out,
but don't wait until you're completely confident to tell
your story.

Wait for her to tie her own shoes,
but don't wait until you're in tip-top shape to run the race.

Wait for the sunset,
but don't wait to say you're sorry.

Wait for the elderly man to shuffle across the street,
but don't wait until you feel "ready" to pursue your dream.

Wait for the hurtful words to dissolve before you speak,
but don't wait to say, "I love you just as you are."

I used to wait on the wrong things.

I used to rush the good things.

I squelched a lot of glorious moments in the process.

Then I started noticing happiness. Happiness on my child's face when I said, "Take your time, baby." Happiness in my soul when I didn't let perfection, fear, or productivity hold me back from living, dreaming, and connecting. Happiness in my daily interactions when I freely gave of my time.

Learning when to wait a moment and when to seize a moment hasn't been easy, but it has changed my life. Happiness came back in.

Today's Reminder

Today I will be aware of moments I tend to rush. I will ask myself, Is it necessary to rush this moment? Will this task or experience be more enjoyable if I give my loved one or myself a bit more time? *If I do decide to give more time, what is the result? Tomorrow I will be aware of moments I need to seize but tend to forgo. I will ask myself,* When I decide to take action, what is the result? *Eventually I hope to be able to better distinguish between when I should wait and when I should go for it.*

29

RENEWAL

We have the power to incorporate elements of a simpler, slower, more natural, and more joy-filled life into our current one if we choose to do so.

THE GIFT OF REAL-LIFE MOMENTS AND CONNECTIONS

Each day I like to envision a future moment when my children are feeding their souls. By imagining them hiking in the woods, talking with a friend, cutting fresh vegetables, closing their eyes in gratitude, and doing what they love most, I am motivated to maintain a clear boundary line between technology and life. I am motivated to provide my children with real-life experiences that involve connecting with nature, service to others, human connection, and pursuing their passions. Preparing my children to seek joy and fulfillment through authentic experiences and meaningful relationships prompts me to actively engage with the world around me and invite my loved ones to come along.

I believe it comes down to this:

If I want my children to experience the freedom that comes from open blue skies and crunchy leaves underfoot, I must partake in such freedoms myself.

If I want my children to appreciate the softness of a beautiful animal, I must take time to appreciate cuddly creatures myself.

If I want my children to relish in the joys of a screen-free Saturday, I must express joy in going off the grid myself.

If I want my children to place less value on things and more value on experiences, I must express delight in music, art, sand castle building, and snowball fights myself.

If I want my children to look straight into the eyes of those who speak to them, I must look into their eyes and listen to their words myself.

I want my children to become aware of the everyday miracles that surround them. Therefore, I must allow time in our daily schedule for us to see and experience them now. Thankfully, drastic life changes are not necessary to do this. I have the power to make our life together simpler, slower, more natural, and more joy-filled if I choose to do so.

If I want my children to seek real-life moments and real-life connections in the future, I must show them that a fulfilling life is grasped with open hands, open eyes, and an open heart in the present.

Today's Reminder

Today our family will schedule a media-free day on the calendar. We will plan to leave our devices at home and go someplace where there are no electronic distractions. We might plan to go on a hike, have a picnic, or visit a museum or a farmers' market. If there is resistance, I will say, "This is important to me." As an adult, I know we need breaks from the digital world. Taking time to unplug is not only a gift to myself but an even greater gift to my children. My children will discover how to experience life with all their senses by watching me do it.

30

New Habits

She stopped getting in the way of Life,
so it could take her by the hand
and point out the sights and sounds she
would have hated to miss.

PUSH IT ALL AWAY

"Life keeps getting in the way," she said,
about shelving her dreams;
about her one-armed hugs;
about her conversations on the run;
about her shortage of relaxation and fun;
about her failure to breathe.
But she was the one putting up the roadblocks—not Life.
She didn't see it at first.
It took one "I can't remember the last time I saw you smile,"
countless declined invitations to play,
and a perpetual feeling of missing out on what really mattered
for her to see, really see.
Then, in a moment of prayerful clarity,
she designated a little time each day to push it all away.
Like a street sweeper, she cleared away the distractions, the excess, and the self-induced pressures to focus on what was right in front of her.

For a few minutes each day, she was free to stop, hold,
listen, love, hope, and breathe.
It was just enough time to realize she wanted more than one
hug a day,
more than one rushed good-bye,
more than one split second to know her precious ones.
So whenever and however she could,
she acted as a street sweeper,
pushing away the roadblocks that kept her from her true path.
She stopped getting in the way of Life
so it could take her by the hand
and point out the sights and sounds she would have hated
to miss.

Today's Reminder

It is easy (and tempting) to allow work, technology, and daily demands to bleed into each other to the point where there are no longer any protected areas. Daily distractions are often invited into the sacred spaces of my life—when I'm behind the wheel of the car, in the bedroom, on Saturday mornings, during family vacations, and even in the middle of the night. Today I will establish designated "work time" and "living time," and find a home base for my devices. These boundary lines will enable me to protect the sacred spaces of my life and breathe life into what matters most.

31

New Habits

*Would it be so bad to do things a little
differently today?
It could mean bringing back something
you've missed dearly.*

WOULD IT BE SO BAD?

Would it be so bad if you skipped washing the dishes in order to cuddle awhile?
It could mean a warm breath upon your cheek.

Would it be so bad if you admitted you made a mistake?
It could mean reconciliation today instead of who knows when.

Would it be so bad if you forgave yourself—really forgave yourself?
It could mean moving on. Finally moving on.

Would it be so bad to be unreachable to the outside world for a bit?
It could mean the most important ones could reach *you*.

Would it be so bad to forgo the extras?
It could mean having the essentials.

Would it be so bad to allow yourself to live and learn?
It could mean your loved ones would offer themselves a little more grace too.

Would it be so bad to loosen your grip on a perfectly orchestrated life?
It could mean embracing a messier but more meaningful one.

Would it be so bad to live a little and laugh a little?
It could mean a smile on your face.
It could mean peace in your heart.
It could mean living, really living, instead of merely existing.

Would it be so bad to do things a little differently today?
It could mean bringing back something you've missed.
That would be good.
Life-enhancing good.
Soul-stirring good.
Day-changing good.

Today's Reminder

It's hard to let go and live when the world is constantly tapping me on the shoulder, reminding me there is so much to be done. But how much I achieved and how fast I responded to the world is not what I want my family to remember about me when I am gone. Today I will let this hopeful truth anchor me: Any act of genuine love or presence (no matter how small or how imperfect) serves as a reset button, drawing me back to what matters most. Let me love my people with the best of me—my heart, my eyes, my ears, my soul. Today let me love them well.

32

New Habits

When it comes to building up a human being,
unconditional attention is just as important
as unconditional love.

THE PEN CAP GESTURE

A few years ago, my dad apologized for being distracted throughout my childhood. "I'm deeply sorry for that," he wrote. "I hope you always knew how much I loved you."

He didn't go into detail about what he was sorry for—he didn't need to. I knew. I remember.

But I remember something more too.

I remember walking across campus to my dad's office every day after school for more than a decade. Upon my arrival I would find my professor father sitting at his desk, surrounded by piles of papers and books. Although the empty chair sitting beside him was probably for a colleague in need of curriculum guidance or a college student seeking scheduling assistance, I always believed that empty chair was for me.

Dad would look up from whatever he was doing and greet me with a smile. Then, as if on cue, he'd place the cap on the black felt-tip pen he used to grade papers or draft notes. The pen cap gesture was my signal. It meant my dad wanted to hear about my day. Sometimes I told him ordinary things. Other times I described something exciting or dramatic that had happened at school. Without fail, my dad would smile as if hearing about *my* day was the best part of *his* day.

This was our routine. From first grade through my senior year in high school, I had after-school chats with my dad.

My dad wasn't perfect. He lost his temper sometimes. He worked too much. He experienced periods of depression. But even through the rough patches, my dad always listened to me. He was never too busy, too distracted, or too desolate to hear my thoughts and opinions.

So despite what the critics say—that giving a child our undivided attention creates a person who thinks the world revolves around him or her—I believe otherwise: **Having a parent who**

listens creates a person who believes he or she has a voice that matters in this world.

In these moments I could have suffered in silence, but instead I spoke up. Why? Because my dad listened to me as I grew.

What this means is there is hope, great hope, for anyone struggling today.

Dear one, perfection is not expected on your parenting journey.

You will have days when you are dealing with heavy, soul-crushing issues.

You will have days when nothing you do seems to be good enough.

You will have days when smiles don't come easy and harsh words are spoken too quickly.

You will have days when you can manage the basics and nothing more.

On those days, I urge you to not say things like, "I am a failure" or "I am a bad parent."

I urge you to, instead, garner the strength, patience, and resolve to do one thing—just one thing:

Listen.

Someday our children will find themselves in difficult situations, and they'll have to choose to suffer in silence or to speak up. Perhaps those will be the moments they will remember our eyes, the nodding of our heads, our thoughtful responses. Suddenly they will be reminded that their voices have value.

That belief can make a life-changing difference.

Today's Reminder

Today I will let someone I love believe that empty chair is just waiting for him or her. Then I will replace the pen cap; turn off the device; set aside my agenda, my guilt, and my regret; and just listen. "I've been looking forward to this time together," I will say. Because when it comes to building up a human being, unconditional attention is as important as unconditional love.

33

Renewal

Maybe second chances are not given to us,
but rather something we offer ourselves
by using new words and new actions.

WHO YOU ARE NOW

Each day I show up—not always calm . . . not always positive . . . not always the person I want to be.

But I remind myself I am not the person I used to be.

You see, there was a time when I wasn't aware I needed improvement.

There was a time when I never would have said, "I'm sorry. I need to adjust my attitude."

There was a time when I beat myself up for past failings, and it would spill out and contaminate my family's day.

Things are different now; I'm not the person I used to be.

Now I live in today. Each moment is a chance to start over. I refuse to let past mistakes sabotage the promise of today.

Take a moment and consider this:

Maybe the words "I'm sorry" can be the start of a freeing dialogue your heart's been yearning to have.

Maybe those you have wronged would be forgiving if you gave them the opportunity.

Maybe second chances are not *given to you*, but rather something you *offer yourself* by using new words and new actions.

Maybe who you are *now* is more important than who you were *then*.

Whether it's been five minutes, five months, or five years since you messed up,

it's not too late to speak words of remorse;

it's not too late to offer forgiveness to those you love, or to yourself;

it's not too late to be the person you always wanted to be;

because who you are now is more important than who you were then.

Who you are now *is more important than who you were then.*

Just think of the gift you'll be giving those who are learning how to live by watching *you* live—not perfectly, but with small, positive steps and daily doses of grace.

Today's Reminder

We have all overreacted. We have all misjudged. We have all done things we regret. We are human, after all. Today I choose to take a step toward healing the hurt caused by my poor choices. I will say or write this to my loved one or myself: "I've given it some thought, and I really wish I'd reacted differently when I _______. I'm sorry for that. Will you forgive me?" In the future I will handle any regrettable actions by apologizing, sharing what I learned from the experience, and saying how I'm going to do things differently next time. Not only will this admission heal the brokenness between us, but it will model something I want my loved ones to do: be human and have the ability to reach out to those they have wronged with remorse, love, and a plan for a better tomorrow.

34

Growth

Speak soul-building words as often as you can so that one day they'll be the strong and steady voice inside your loved one's heart.

SOUL-BUILDING WORDS

"I will wait for you."
"Take your time."
"You make my day better."
I say those words to my slow-moving, happy-go-lucky, noticer-of-life child.
I watch as grateful eyes light up and tiny shoulders relax.
Those words are soul-building words to her.

"Mistakes mean you are learning."
"Okay, you can have a few more minutes to work on your project."
"You wanted it to be just right, didn't you?"
I say those words to my driven, conscientious pursuer-of-dreams child.
I watch as pressure escapes from her chest and future aspirations come closer.
Those words are confidence-boosting words to her.

"I appreciate you."
"I'm listening."
"You matter."
I say those words to the hard-working, often underappreciated love of my life.
I watch as tensions loosen, eyes meet mine, and conversation comes more easily.
Those words are affirming and connecting words to him.

"It's good enough for today."
"I'm doing the best I can right now."
"Only love today."

I say those words to my own perfection-seeking, worrying heart.
I watch as my clenched hands open. Tears fall as scars come
to the surface.
Those are healing, hope-filled words to me.

The words "I love you" should never be underestimated, but every human being has a few words that make her soul come alive, that bring peace to his uncertain heart, that help them rise when they fall. Discover what those words are by watching. What makes her smile? What motivates him to keep trying? What adds a spring to his step? Commit those soul-building words to memory and say them as often as you can so that one day they'll be the strong and steady voice inside your loved one's heart.

Today's Reminder

Like sunlight to a plant, some words nourish the deepest parts of the human heart and foster growth in all areas of life. That's why they are called soul-building words. *Today I will commit some to memory and say them to my loved ones as often as I can.*

35

New Habits

One empty box.
One six-second action.
Let the living begin.

THE SIX-SECOND CHALLENGE

In six seconds you can kiss someone like you mean it.
In six seconds you can hold open a door.

In six seconds you can wait for a little straggler to catch up.
"I'll wait for you," you can even say.

In six seconds you can take a deep breath.
In six seconds you can decide it's not worth it and let it go.
In six seconds you can tuck a note in a lunch box or in a pocket. It takes two seconds to draw a heart.

In six seconds you can say you're sorry.
In six seconds you can cut yourself some slack.
In six seconds you can throw away that picture, that pair of pants, that inner bully that keeps you from loving this day, this you.

In six seconds you can feel the sunshine.
In six seconds you can decide it's time to stop looking back.
In six seconds you can whisper, "It's gonna be okay," to yourself or someone who's scared.

In six seconds you can drop a dollar into a hat.
In six seconds you can pick up that old guitar.
In six seconds you can look into someone's eyes and say, "My life is better because of you."

I used to sound like a broken record.
"I don't have time," I'd always say.
But then I realized what could happen in a mere six seconds.
It's enough to make a bad day good.
It's enough to bring life back to your weary bones.
It's enough to remember what really matters in the midst of so much that doesn't.

Today's Reminder

Having empathy for others increases my empathy for myself. If I find myself judging or criticizing someone, I will imagine for a moment the unseen burdens he or she is carrying. Whether it's someone I love, someone I work with, or a complete stranger, acknowledging another's unseen burdens creates compassion—not just for them, but also for me. I will ease pressure in and around me by extending compassion rather than judgment. Putting that compassion into a six-second action can change everything. Putting that compassion into a six-second action can change the world.

36

Renewal

Today is too precious not to be lived all *the way.*
Let's decide there's no sitting down for this.

LIVING ALL THE WAY

When my nephew was very small, he'd hold up his arms and say, "Hold you all the way."

It was his way of asking any willing adult to pick him up and then stand up. It meant there was no sitting down for this.

Remembering that got me thinking of all the things—the important things—I choose to do halfway instead of all the way.

Consider this with me:

What would it mean to *listen* all the way?

It would mean paying attention to her words but also to her inflection and tone. It would mean making the person in front of me feel seen, heard, and valued.

What would it mean to *love* all the way?

It would mean hugging hard, hugging long, and not being the first to let go. It would mean looking past his flaws and imperfections to see an everyday miracle.

What would it mean to *respect myself* all the way?

It would mean forgiving myself on a daily basis. It would mean seeing myself with kind eyes and talking to myself with gentle words. It would mean loving myself as is.

What would it mean to *forgive* all the way?

It would mean letting go of grudges and being the first to say, "I'm sorry." It would mean living in today and not in the past. It would mean a soft place to lay my head at night.

What would it mean to *feel* all the way?

It would mean resisting the urge to let myself go numb, to hide my feelings, and to hide my pain. It would mean baring my soul to a trusted friend. It would mean giving an honest answer when someone asks, "How are you?"

What would it mean to *hope* all the way?

It would mean trusting—trusting that within the challenges I face, there are opportunities to learn, grow, and come out stronger on the other side. It would mean anticipating a moment of goodness will be upon me if I just keep looking.

What would it mean to *breathe* all the way?

It would mean pausing regularly. It would mean noticing the sun on my face, the softness of my pet's fur, the sound of my beloved's laughter. It would mean having peaceful pockets within my frenzied day.

What would it mean to *live* all the way?

It would mean pursuing the passions of my heart and paying no mind to the naysayers. It would mean laughing out loud and enjoying every bite of that decadent dessert. It would mean filling my hands and heart with what matters most.

As you face a new day, will you experience it halfway or all the way?

You can decide today is too precious not to be lived *all* the way. You can decide there's no sitting down for this.

Today's Reminder

I will do one thing all the way today. Perhaps it's something small—to savor each sip of my coffee or walk to the mailbox fully aware of the sky, wind, and trees. Perhaps it's something big—such as putting away the scale or finding forgiveness. I will see how doing this one thing all the way *impacts my soul and my outlook. I will see how this one small investment fuels me forward.*

37

New Habits

I am starting to see that my days are made up of a million little choices—choices to grasp the things that really matter or let them slip through my busy fingers.

The Right Choice

"Name twenty things you love about me," Avery said just as I was shutting the door to her bedroom.

I immediately thought about the dirty dishes in the sink, the work I had yet to do, and the ache in my back, and I almost said, "Not tonight."

But I didn't.

Instead, I slowly made my way back to her bed and rattled off things such as, "I love your smile . . . I love the way you sing . . . I love how you help your friends . . . I love the way you make me laugh . . . I love the way you take your time . . . I love your strong hugs . . ."

I made it to twenty quite quickly, and I watched the smile on her face get a little wider with each reason I listed.

"Thank you, Mama. I love how you love me," Avery said as she rolled over, preparing to sleep.

It took less than one minute, this little request of hers, but there is a good chance she will remember this list, this very important list.

I don't always get it right. I don't.

But I am starting to see that my days are made up of a million little choices—choices to grasp the things that really matter or let them slip through my busy fingers.

Last night I chose the girl who still stands on her tiptoes to reach the sink.

Last night I chose the girl who still likes me to read bedtime stories to her or hold her hand in the parking lot.

Last night I chose the girl who sings made-up songs while offering me dandelion bouquets.

Last night I chose the girl with the wiggly teeth and contagious laugh.

With the kitchen in disarray and a hundred things to do, I chose my child. Because I still can. Today my child stands before me wanting, needing, and hoping to be chosen. Tomorrow might be different.

Today's Reminder

Just because I'm in the midst of a challenge doesn't mean I can't keep moving forward. Tiny steps count. Just because I face a giant obstacle doesn't mean I should let it get in the way of living. Small actions make a difference. Just because I'm not out of the woods doesn't mean I should stop looking for the sun. Minuscule efforts light the path. Today offers one empty box in the calendar of life. I will use it to perform one positive action that makes my heart come alive and connects me to what (or who) matters most.

— II —

Summer: Shining Through

Authenticity, Connection, and Acceptance

When we see each other's scars,
we love each other more.

When my friend lost her sister to cancer, she astounded me with one simple act. She talked about it—the pain and disbelief, the pressure to move on, the things that helped and the things that didn't. She talked about the good days and the nearly indescribable bad days.

Each time my friend shared her struggles, triumphs, and truths, I was struck with admiration and awe. She never wanted to be an expert on grief, but she is. She never wanted to know what words and actions bring a moment of solace to an aching soul, but she does. This was now my friend's story, and as much as she wanted to deny it, she was choosing to own it by revealing it to the world through her life's window.

I thought of my friend and her authentic window display when I had to have a CT scan on my abdomen. It was the first time I'd lain beneath such a big, scary machine, and I held my breath for dear life. As the machine began to slowly inch my body under the camera, I thought of my friend and her story. I wasn't sure how my story was going to play out, but I decided I'd display truth in my life's window. I'd tell my close friends what was happening. I'd say, "I'm scared" when I needed comfort. I'd ask for help when I was in pain. Based on my friend's example, I knew it was important to pay attention. Whether I liked it or not, I was gaining valuable insight that might one day inspire connection, action, or relief when placed in my life's window. I vowed to take it all in—the good as well as the bad—and perhaps discover something worth sharing in the process.

One month after the CT scan that saved my left kidney and possibly my life, I was home from the hospital. I was swollen and sore. I was groggy from pain meds. I was having trouble thinking of words. I was kind of a mess, but I had something I needed to say. I pulled my computer gingerly onto my lap and typed a message to my friends and family on social media. I remember worrying for a brief moment about incomplete sentences, misspelled words, and extra periods. The words were blurry to my grateful, teary eyes, but I clicked "post" anyway. This is what I wrote:

> *I am home from the hospital recovering from kidney surgery and feeling incredibly thankful to be here. It's been many months of infection and uncertainty, but I finally have peace. I am on my way to more years, more love, more life. My little public service announcement in the midst of this overwhelming gratitude is this: If you feel that something is not right in your body or mind, please don't dismiss that feeling. Make an appointment today. If you are not satisfied with the answers you get or things do not improve, keep searching. Keep asking. Keep listening. Keep going until you get answers. You are the only one who can truly look after* you. *And your people need you to be here.*

An interesting thing happened. Two of my neighbors contacted me over the next few weeks to tell me those words prompted them to action. One of them made an appointment regarding a persistent pain she'd neglected to look into. Another friend said she'd been worried about her spouse's health, and my words were the perfect ones to gently nudge him into action.

I cried with relief. Had I chosen to keep my experience to

myself because of potential flaws or my fear of judgment, these critical human connections and life-saving actions wouldn't have happened. In that moment, my life's window opened wide. The light left nothing hidden. What was revealed was far from perfect, but it was not unsightly; it was beautiful because it invited others to bravely open their windows too.

Around the same time, as I lay in my bed recovering, Avery came to my room with a package from my publisher. It was the very first copy of my second book, *Hands Free Life*, soon to be released into the world.

"Will you read it to me?" she asked, curling up next to me in bed.

I hesitated. The book held many truths about the overly critical and highly distracted woman I once was. There were things this child did not know about me, and I wasn't sure I wanted her to know them—at least not that day.

"How about this page?" She turned to page 105.

With reluctance, I began to read about a joyless woman who unexpectedly found hope in a smudged handprint on the sunroof of her car. Strapped in a booster seat in those days, Avery had borne witness to my angry departures over a distressing two-year period. But she did not remember the fear in her sister's eyes, the slamming doors, or my impatient demands to "hurry up." But that particular day—the day I pulled over to show my daughters a sea of white clouds—was different. *I* was different. Avery's little handprint against a cloud-saturated backdrop served as a providential compass, pointing me back to joy.

When I finished reading, I quietly closed the crisp new book, unable to look my child in the eyes. I'm not sure if I was expecting her to look at me with shock, disappointment, or disdain, but I was holding my breath until she spoke.

"I *love* you, Mama," she said, emphasizing the word *love*. Then she cuddled up against me, and we sat in silent reflection.

When we see each other's scars, we love each other more.

I'd written that line five years prior. But it hadn't truly come to life until that moment as I exposed my scars and truths to the one person I most wanted to hide them from. Through my friend's devastating loss and my current health struggles, I'd realized I didn't want to waste my precious days putting anything fake in my life's window. By displaying my true self, I might inspire those around me to display their true selves as well. What a gift it is to meet others in the light of realness, a place where we can love each other even *more* because of our shared imperfections, vulnerabilities, and experiences.

When we see each other's scars, we love each other more. This is what I believe. I believe it for my friend, who's mourning the loss of her sister while bravely creating an authentic window display vastly different from the one she planned on. I believe it for my child, who's in the early stages of planning her window display. I believe it for myself, a woman who's using her mistakes as stepping-stones to becoming the best version of herself. I believe it for you, no matter how messy, painful, complicated, or unfinished your current situation is.

Perhaps you sit here with a messy story you haven't shared. Maybe you thought it had to be all figured out before you told someone. Maybe you thought it had to have a happy ending before it could be revealed. Maybe you thought you had to have periods in all the right places for it to be seen.

I hope and pray you come to see it differently.

By bravely sharing your experiences, hopes, dreams, and imperfections, you have the power to encourage those around you to live boldly, authentically, and confidently. It is not easy, I know. Revealing your true self to others and accepting them "as is" takes time, practice, patience, and opportunity. It is a blessing to provide these window openers to you in the season ahead. Each one offers a chance to embrace yourself, scars and all, a chance to love your people exactly as they are, an invitation to step into the forgiving light of realness and make room for others to join you there.

Let's take our first step toward revealing our truest selves and giving others the same gift. Let's open wide our life's windows and let the forgiving light of authenticity, connection, and acceptance heal us in ways unimagined.

1

AUTHENTICITY

In the act of waiting until, we delay the true living of life.

REAL LIVING FOUND HERE

Help Wanted, read the sign in the shop window.
This got me thinking.
What about the signs we put in the windows of our lives?
Perfection Wanted, read too many of them.
That's why I can't submit my story for publication.
My story needs more work.
I'll just keep working on it.

That's why I can't invite friends over to my house.
My house isn't fully furnished.
I'll just wait until I get a sofa.

That's why I can't voice my opinion on the issue.
I can't find the right words.
I'll just keep thinking about it until the perfect words come
to me.

That's why I can't take my kids to that class they'd love.
They might act up.
I'll wait until we get our issues sorted out.

That's why I don't pick up that instrument.
I can practice only once a week.
I'll pick it up when I have more free time.

That's why I don't exercise.
I can't take the stairs without getting winded.
I'll start being more active when I have more energy.

Perfection Wanted.
We hang those words in the windows of our lives, and in that act of *waiting until*,
we delay the true living of life.

Sure, you might not get published.
Sure, you might scare someone away with your dust bunnies.
Sure, the kids might act up and embarrass you.
Sure, you might stutter or play the wrong notes.
But what if those things don't matter?
What if someone looks out her window and sees you putting one foot in front of the other?
What if your decision to tear up your Perfection Wanted sign inspires someone to tear up his?

You have the power to change the sign you are hanging in the window of your life.
Why not this instead?
Adventure Wanted.
Grace Wanted.

Authenticity Wanted.
Real Living Wanted—and found here.

Today's Reminder

Today I am putting up a new sign in the window of my life. It reads: __________ Wanted. I will describe what it might look like in my life and figure out one small step I can take to make it happen. Then I will welcome ___________ into my life with arms wide open. I will ask it to stay, to take up permanent residence in my soul.

2

Acceptance

Don't change, extraordinary one.
You're gonna light up this place.

DON'T CHANGE, EXTRAORDINARY ONE

They say he's too quiet.
They say she's too inquisitive.
They say he's too energetic.
They say she's too sensitive.
They say these things thinking it will help,
but it doesn't.
It only causes worry and the pressure to conform.
The truth is, changing would be a tragedy.

Because when they say "too quiet,"
I see introspection.

Don't change, thoughtful one.
You're gonna bring quiet wisdom to the chaos.

Because when they say "too inquisitive,"
I see problem solving.
Don't change, little thinker.
You're gonna to bring answers to the toughest questions.

Because when they say "too energetic,"
I see vitality.
Don't change, lively one.
You're gonna bring love and laughter to desperate times.

Because when they say "too sensitive,"
I see heart.
Don't change, deep feeler.
You're gonna bring compassion to hurting souls.

Because when they say "too anxious,"
I see caution.
Don't change, little protector.
You're gonna bring deliberation to tricky situations.

They might say change is needed.
I ask that they look a little deeper and observe a little longer.
From where I stand, these individuals are just as they should be—
On their path to bring the world exactly what it needs to thrive.

Don't change, extraordinary one.
You're gonna light up this place.

Today's Reminder

Today I will consider that "problem" characteristic in a new way. Perhaps that weakness is strength in need of a little nurturing and some direction. I will try to discover the strengths hidden in "problem areas" that one day might be a gift to the world.

3

Acceptance

I am more than one opinion, one poor
choice, or one Saturday night mistake.
I am more than I give myself credit for.

MAYBE IT'S TIME

I wish I were beautiful.
Maybe you are.

I wish I were smart.
Who's to say you're not?

I wish I were brave.
Perhaps it's there, just waiting to be seen.

I wish I could start over.
Why not today?

I wish I could do a better job at this.
Maybe this is your do-over moment.

I wish I could see the light at the end of the tunnel.
Maybe that first glimmer will come when you least expect it.

I wish I could love myself.
Maybe it's time.

Maybe it's time to unload the heavy, hurtful words and preconceived notions you've carried around for too long.
Perhaps enough is enough.
Who says you aren't worthy of love, acceptance, and peace?
Maybe someone does,
but don't let that someone be you.

You are more than one opinion, one poor choice, or one Saturday night mistake.
You are more than you give yourself credit for.

Instead of going further down the damaging path of "I am not," consider lifting yourself up with "I am" and "I can."
I am beautiful.
I am smart.
I am brave.
I can start over.
I am doing the best I can.
I can see the light at the end of the tunnel.
I can love myself.
I am more than one opinion, one poor choice, or one Saturday night mistake.
I am more than I give myself credit for.
I am more than I am not.

Today's Reminder

Today I start being kind to myself. I will begin with one powerful action: I will post positive notes from loved ones or inspiring quotes in my home. They will serve as visual reminders to see myself through loving eyes and speak to myself as I would a dear friend. By making it a habit to extend kindness and compassion to myself, I will be better able to extend patience and kindness to others. In time, positive and uplifting words will be routine for me because they will reflect the change in my heart.

4

Connection

In a world quick to condemn, criticize,
and overreact, be quick to be kind.

ONE KIND THING

The summer before I started middle school, I gained a lot of weight and developed unsightly stretch marks on my thighs. I was ashamed. While my parents worked during the day, my older sister took me to the neighborhood pool. I braced myself when I walked out of the changing stall. My sister never said one word about my body. She only said, "I love your bathing suit!" I remember as if it were yesterday. It meant everything that she managed to think of one nice thing when she could have said something cruel or nothing at all.

In the days that followed, other people were not so kind, but the pain was eased by remembering what my sister said. She'd said one nice thing, and her opinion mattered more than all the others.

Although my sister was very smart, and had long, beautiful hair and good conversation skills, I realized that anyone could be that person—the person who thinks of one nice thing when no one else does.

From that moment, I set a secret goal to be the person who thought of one nice thing—especially when I noticed someone looking uncomfortable, insecure, or left out. Those people were easy to spot. They always looked a little sad or a little angry. Saying one nice thing almost always brought a look of relief. Sometimes it started a conversation; other times it didn't, but I always loved seeing that tiny flash of relief. As an elementary education major in college, I got to visit many classrooms. I was always drawn to the children whose desks were pulled away from everyone else's. I would bend down and ask a few questions. As the child began to talk, a compliment would pop into my head. When I said it, the child would always look at me a little funny—as if perhaps he hadn't heard anything nice about himself in a while. That is when I knew what God was calling me to do with my life.

I went on to be a special education teacher. I always appreciated the children who would take a moment to talk to, encourage, or include my students. I would later pull those kind children aside and tell them how that one nice thing they said or did made a difference. "I don't think I've ever seen my student smile like that," I would say. Or "I'm certain she's going to remember your kindness forever." The children would look surprised and pleased and then go on giving more kindness as if it was their job.

Now that I have children of my own, I encourage them to be the person who thinks of one nice thing. I don't think there is a more important person to be. I say:

Yeah, it might be cool to be the one who knows all the answers, but consider being the one who thinks of one nice thing.

Yeah, it might be cool to be the one invited to all the parties, but consider being the one who shows up when no one else does.

Yeah, it might be cool to be the one everyone gathers around, but consider being the one who extends an invitation to someone outside the circle.

Yeah, it might be cool to be the one with all the latest gadgets, but consider being the one who always has something kind to say.

Be that one. The look of relief on another person's face is far better than any trophy, any contest, any invitation, or any award.

In a world quick to condemn, criticize, and overreact, be quick to be kind.

Your kindness might just be carried in someone's heart forever, changing the course of her life for good.

Today's Reminder

Today I want to be a compliment giver. I want to be a grocery cart returner. I want to be a door holder. I want to be an elevator button pusher who says, "What floor do you need?" I want to be a bathroom counter wiper and a trash picker upper. I want to leave people and places better than the way I found them. I want to represent courtesy and love. I want to look back and feel satisfied at the way I am leaving the world around me.

5

Acceptance

Today I will take a page from your book—
your very wise and compassionate book that
my grown-up self could learn a lot from.

A PAGE FROM YOUR BOOK

I drop the ball.
I grump through my day.
I act without thinking.
But because I am an adult, no one calls me on it.

I say things I shouldn't.
I forget—a lot.
I stumble, and sometimes I fall on my face.
But because I am grown up, no one points fingers.

I eat too quickly.
I don't wait very well.
I don't always make the best choices.
But because I am big, no one corrects me.
Not even you, the one who sees me at my worst.

When I mess up, you don't keep track.
When I lose my cool, you don't send me to my room.
When I fail, you don't let out an exasperated sigh.
You hug me and say, "Everybody makes mistakes."
I don't give second chances like I should.
But you do.
You always do.
Even when I don't deserve them.

So maybe next time you drop the ball, or grump through your day, or act without thinking, I will take a page from your book—your very wise and compassionate book that my grown-up self could learn a lot from.

Today's Reminder

It's far too easy to be impatient and unkind to the ones I love because I know they'll always love me—but shouldn't I be most kind *to those who love me no matter how poorly I've behaved? Shouldn't I be* most tender *to those who wipe my tears? Shouldn't I be* most generous *to those who tend to my deepest needs? Life is more livable when we embrace our humanness and remember we are all just learning and doing the best we know how.*

6

Authenticity

Even though it's broken, it's still beautiful.

YOU'RE A KEEPER

"Even though it's broken, it's still beautiful," my child said, placing the fractured seashell in her bucket. It was a keeper, even though it was broken.

That got me thinking. How quickly we discard ourselves—the part of us that is beautiful despite our flaws and failings.

What if we were to see ourselves through kinder eyes—eyes that see the whole picture, not just the weaknesses?

It might sound like this:

Even though I am exhausted, I am still here.
Even though I was late, I still showed up.
Even though I burned dinner, I still provided.
Even though I am not the size I want to be, I am still worthy.
Even though I didn't have the answers, I still offered my presence.
Even though I didn't express myself perfectly, I still had a voice that mattered.
Even though I got lost for a while, I still found my way.
Even though I am broken at times, I still love my family wholeheartedly.

It's critical to see *all you are* rather than what's missing, imperfect, unattractive, or broken.

You see, there's someone who looks at you and sees something he or she can hold on to.

You're a keeper.

Keep keepin' on.

Today's Reminder

Today I will not push myself to unrealistic standards. I will tell myself, "It's good enough for today." Perhaps, in time, those words will evolve into, "I am enough today." As I go about my day, I will shift my focus from where I fall short to where I triumph (even the tiniest positives are noteworthy). I vow to be in my own corner today. I might be a little faded and cracked, but I am a "keeper," worthy of love and celebration.

7

Acceptance

Because of you, there is a human being walking on this earth who doesn't have to ask for love—it is just given.

YOU LOVE THEM ANYWAY

Someone you love might be extra sensitive today.
Someone you love might wear a permanent scowl.
Someone you love might be eerily quiet or unreasonably defensive.
And you love her anyway.

Someone you love might not want to talk.
Someone you love might be trying to shut you out.

Someone you love might be trying to push you away.
And you love him anyway.

Someone you love might say hateful words.
Someone you love might hate herself right now.
Someone you love might hate you right now.
And you love her anyway.

Someone you love might not be himself right now.
Someone you love might be really hard to love right now.
Someone you love might feel very far away.
And you love him anyway.
And you love her anyway.

Just let that soak in for a moment.
You love someone at his worst.
You love someone when she's most unlovable.
You love them anyway.
You love them anyway.

Your love is stronger than any foul mood, any bad attitude, and any poor choice. And no matter how hard your someone is to love at times, you find a way to do it.

Your love always finds a way.

Just let that soak in for a moment.

Oh, I know there are things you need to work on. Me too. But your love—that comforting presence your someone can count on—is more significant than perhaps you ever realized.

Because of you, there is a human being walking on this earth who doesn't have to ask for love—it is just given.

Because of you, there is a human being who doesn't have to wonder if he is loved. He just knows.

Because of you, someone can be human—with faults, flaws, moods, and mistakes—and still be loved.

There is no greater gift in someone's lifetime than unconditional, never-failing, steadfast love.

Let that soak in, and put your doubts and failings to rest.

Then go on doing what you do best: loving them.

Today's Reminder

Each time I take a difficult look inward and think about how I can listen, communicate, and nurture my people better, that is a significant act of love. I will carry this hope-filled truth with me today as I make mistakes, stumble, fall, and get back up. I will remember to look at the love I offer again and again. My offerings of love matter more than the mistakes I make.

8

Connection

I want to love you by your book and witness the unfolding of your amazing story.

I Want to Love You by Your Book: A Daily Pledge

I will study you. I will listen to you. I will watch your face when I use certain words or tones. What brings a smile to your face? What causes embarrassment or shame? I will take note. I will use words that build you up instead of words that break you down. When I see that something I do makes you feel uncomfortable or rejected, I will remember and try not to do it again.

I want to love you by your book.

I will have one-on-one time with you, even if this means having to make personal sacrifices or disappoint people outside our family. Making time to know you may mean declining extra commitments or reducing extracurricular activities. It may mean watching a television show I don't care for or being willing to learn about your hobbies. It may mean sitting beside you in silence. I pledge to be available to you. I pledge to show you you're worth my time and attention.

I want to love you by your book.

I will tell you all the positive things I notice about you, instead of pointing out where you fall short. There are enough people who will catch you falling short in your lifetime. I will be your encourager. I will be your number one fan. I want to hear you laugh. I want to see you smile. I want to watch you shine.

I want to love you by your book and witness the unfolding of your amazing story.

Today's Reminder

Today I will listen with my eyes, ears, and heart when my beloved people speak. Listening attentively to my loved ones' dreams, needs, and questions results in the ability to know *them. And when a person feels known, they feel loved and understood in the most powerful way possible.*

9

Acceptance

There's something quite beautiful about a song in its natural, imperfect form—a lot like the light of joy that radiates on a child's face when loved "as is."

TO LOVE "AS IS"

I remember the moment I first saw the importance of loving my child "as is." Avery was practicing her ukulele for a recital that was just days away. Her notes were off-key. Her pick was making an annoying clicking noise as she strummed. I kept making her play it again, hoping it would get better. Finally, after several more arduous renditions, my child simply laid down her instrument as if surrendering to an unwinnable battle. I will never forget her words as long as I live.

"Mama, I just want to be good," Avery said as a tear ran down each cheek.

My baby, who was trying the best she could to play a complicated instrument, thought she was no good. The act of playing the ukulele, something that had initially brought her so much joy, was now a source of frustration and failure. What she once called her "special gift" was now something she felt she did poorly.

Where could she have gotten that idea? Could it have been from all the disapproving looks and constant corrections? Could it have been from the exasperated sighs coming from the unsmiling lady standing over her?

I never wanted my child to think she was only as good as her accomplishments. I wanted her self-worth to come from who she is, not what she does. Yet that was not the message I had been conveying over the course of our practice sessions.

I cradled my daughter in my arms and told her how sorry I was. In that moment, I vowed to simply let her play her beloved ukulele with no expectations, no pressure—just play to her heart's content. Now we sit on the front step, and she plays to the birds without any sheet music. The birds don't seem to mind the out-of-tune notes, and neither do I. There's something quite beautiful about a song in its natural, imperfect form—it's a lot like the light of joy that radiates on a child's face when she is loved "as is."

Today's Reminder

Seeing my children as human beings with thoughts, feelings, ideas, hopes, and dreams motivates me to periodically reconsider my parental expectations. Are they reasonable? Realistic? Necessary? Age appropriate? Frequently evaluating and modifying my expectations cultivates a home in which positives are noticed, strengths are nurtured, and unconditional love is abundant.

10

Acceptance

The world might try to tell you that you
don't fit in. I beg to differ;
I think you are the missing piece.

To the Precious Soul Yearning to Fit In

If you find yourself towering over others, don't slouch to fit in with the rest;
stand tall and admire the view from up there.

If you find yourself wishing you didn't have to wear glasses,
go funky with the frames and notice the details of life you might've missed.

If you find yourself wishing you didn't take up so much of the seat,
know that the person sitting next to you thinks she's lucky to be your friend.

If you find your dreams so outlandish no one believes you can achieve them,
keep moving forward with quiet determination, because you know something they don't.

If you find yourself diminishing under the weight of popular opinion,
don't listen to random voices; listen to the one voice you can trust.

If you find your colors so different you're unable to blend in,
realize that chartreuse and violet are desperately needed in a black-and-white world.

If you find yourself wondering if it'll always be this hard,
envision the moment when all the tears you've cried and all the obstacles you've faced allow you to look into someone's eyes and say, "I've been where you are; you're gonna make it."

Dear one, your existence is too vital for you to fade into a crowd. Your purpose is too important to be squelched by doubt and fear. Your colors are too vibrant to hide.

Each time you boldly step forward and say, "This is who I am," a piece of our broken world falls into place.

The world might try to tell you that you don't fit in.

I beg to differ.

I think you are the missing piece.

This world is not complete without you.

Today's Reminder

Today I will refuse to hide my unique colors in order to blend in. I will embrace the unique colors I see in others. I will be sure my beloved people know I love them just as they are, exactly as they are.

11

Connection

You are more than enough.
You are living proof that a person's soul
becomes more colorful
with each stumble, with each fall, and with
each try, try again.

YOU ARE ENOUGH

You didn't make the team.
You're still enough for me.

You didn't get the part.
You're still enough for me.

You didn't get the job.
You're still enough for me.

You didn't make the cut.
You're still enough for me.

You didn't choose the right words.
You're still enough for me.

You didn't meet expectations.
You're still enough for me.

You're still enough.
You're still enough.
Let me tell you why:
You almost gave up, but you didn't.
Your buttons were pushed, but you kept your cool.
You found it challenging, but you kept trying.
You could've left in a huff, but you stayed.
You could've looked away, but you spoke up.
You could've denied, but you confessed.
You got nothing in return, but you gave anyway.
You were off-key, but you still sang your heart out.

You are enough.
You are more than enough.
You are living proof that with each stumble,
with each fall,
with each try, try again,
a new color is added to your vibrant soul.
Keep trying. Keep shining. You are enough.

Today's Reminder

Given our achievement-driven culture, it's easy to get caught up in numbers, evaluations, statistics, awards, and wins. But I don't want to forget about compassion, integrity, kindness, determination, courage, and honesty. I don't want to squelch the happiness my loved ones feel when they're doing what they love. Placing less emphasis on grades, goals, and appearance and instead noticing acts of bravery, effort, and authenticity allows joy to be present, no matter the score.

12

AUTHENTICITY

The life with the battle scars, the imperfections, and the bruises is the one I want to live—and the life I want to embrace when I see it in others.

THE SIGN OF AUTHENTICITY

For a long time, I didn't let anyone in on how I really felt or who I really was. I plastered on a smile even when I was sad, empty, overwhelmed, or scared. The sign I put in my window was PERFECTION. I sacrificed authenticity because I thought showing the world who I really was would drive people away. I've since learned showing our true selves (flaws and all) is what draws people toward us, not what pushes them away.

Unfortunately, it took me almost forty years to get it. I don't want anyone I love to have to hide their truest self from the world for one more day. I had a chance to tell this to my daughter in a way she could understand and remember as she grows.

What I See in the Window of Your Life

I see the sign TENACITY each time you admit you've made a mistake and try to do better. May you always see failures as stepping-stones and opportunities for growth.

I see the sign SELF-ASSURANCE each time you wear your own personal style regardless of the latest trend. May you always accept yourself and not rely on acceptance from others.

I see the sign ASSERTIVENESS when you say, "No thanks, I'm good," when a friend asks you to do something you don't want to do. May you always be able to speak up for yourself and do what's best for you.

I see the sign VULNERABILITY when you are struggling and ask for help. May you always surround yourself with people who love you, care for you, and want to help you succeed. May you always be strong enough to say, "I need help."

I see the sign CAPABILITY when you tackle Grandma's biscuit recipe, wash and fold your laundry, and buy gifts with your own money. May you always find fulfillment in doing things for yourself rather than in having them done for you.

My child, as you grow and experience changes in body, mind, and friendships, it will not always be easy to share your truest self. Therefore, count on me to support your authenticity in these ways:

When you say you aren't hungry, I am not going to try to convince you otherwise.

When you say someone makes you feel uncomfortable, I will respect that feeling and help you keep your distance. I will also ask questions to make sure you are safe.

When you ask me not to tell anyone about an embarrassing moment or foolish mistake, I won't.

When you say, "I'd rather not spend the night at the slumber party, but can I stay until ten o'clock?" I will say yes.

When you say you know the best way to complete a school project, I will stand back and let you do it, even if it looks like it might not work out.

Whether it's placing your order at a restaurant or announcing a lifelong goal, I will respect your voice and opinion.

I will admire the truths you display in your window, even if they are different from mine.

When you speak truths about yourself that are hard for me to hear, I will not turn away. I will open my arms and remember how I felt when finally, at last, I let someone in on mine. Six years ago, I admitted a painful truth I'd never told a soul. I said, "I feel like a failure." My friend whispered back, "Me too." And there, as the most authentic versions of ourselves, we found a common thread that connected us and gave us hope.

When we see each other's scars, we love each other more.

This is what I believe.

The life with the nicks, scratches, scars, and imperfections displayed in the window—that's the life I want to walk into, the life I want to live, the life I want to embrace when I see it in others.

When I do, I will celebrate that momentous display of human courage by opening my arms and saying, "Me too."

Today's Reminder

The truths and insecurities we feel most inclined to keep to ourselves are the ones that should be vocalized. This is when the lines of our stories become lyrics to an anthem of hope, love, and acceptance. Today I will speak one true emotion or detail about my life to a trusted friend or loved one. Being real with this person increases the chance she or he will be real with me. What a gift it is to meet each other in the light of realness.

13

Acceptance

To wonder about you is to know you, to see
you, to delight in you just as you are.
To wonder about you is to love you in the
most empowering way possible.

YOU ARE A WONDER

When it comes to my loved one's future,
I cannot predict. So let me stop.

I cannot accelerate. So let me pause.

I cannot control. So let me release.

But there is something I *can* do. There is something we can all do to celebrate our loved ones for who they are now, rather than what their current skills or interests indicate they might become.

We can wonder.

To wonder about you is to know you, to see you, to delight in you just as you are.

To wonder about you is to love you in the most empowering way possible.

Today I invite you to join me in the *act of wondering* in an effort to enhance futures rather than diminish them. Take a look:

To the child who'd rather catch butterflies than fly balls . . .
to the child who wants to play catch 'til the sun goes down . . .
You are a wonder.

To the child who prefers solitude . . .
to the child who prefers an audience . . .
You are a wonder.

To the child who does things in her own way, in her own time . . .
to the child who forges ahead with no sign of slowing down . . .
You are a wonder.

To the child who wears his heart on his sleeve . . .
to the child who wears a costume to the supermarket . . .
You are a wonder.

To the child whose butterfly colors light up a room . . .
to the child whose firefly light shines quietly from within . . .

You are a wonder.

To the child who questions everything about life . . .
to the child whose inherent knowledge runs deep . . .
You are a wonder.

So go on, extraordinary one.
Live and let live.
Love and be loved.
Bloom in time—in your own time.
Now I see you for who you really are.
And you are a wonder.
I'm sorry I didn't see it before.
I see it now.
I see it now.
You are a wonder.
I'll be watching proudly with glistening eyes to see what
your future holds.

Today's Reminder

Today I will love my people "as is." Instead of harping on their bad habits, low marks, messy rooms, or future pursuits, I will pause and simply marvel at who they are at this very moment. In that sacred pause I take to marvel, there'll be room to for love and acceptance to come in.

14

Connection

Today could be about being human—being
that pretty amazing human who lives
inside these walls.

ABOUT BEING HUMAN

Today could be about the cleanliness of his room,
or it could be about noticing the way his eyes sparkle when
you say his name with love.

Today could be about pushing her glasses up on her nose,
or it could be about feeling the force of her hug when you
are united.

Today could be about remembering to leave shoes by
the door,
or it could be about leaving the door open for questions,
laughter, conversation.

Today could be about the holes in his socks,
or it could be about making space in the midst of the day's
duties to hear his words.

Today could be about what place she took in the race,
or it could be about the spot she always saves for that shy,
awkward friend.

Today could be about the lack of positive check marks,
or it could be about the admirable qualities not measured on
a school report.

Today could be about what he is not doing, not thinking,
and not achieving,
or it could be about what he does that makes you feel
amazed and proud.

Today could be about what she's going to make of herself,
or it could be about who she already is—who she already
awesomely is.

Today could be about our agendas, our standards, our
timelines,
or it could be about their efforts, their thoughts, their
feelings, their hopes, their dreams.

Today could be about expectations, pressure, and
perfection—but then again, there's enough of that
outside these walls.
Today could be about being human—being that pretty
amazing human who lives inside these walls.
And today could be a good day to tell her so.

Today's Reminder

Today I will be less of a critic and more of an encourager. I will make a conscious effort to notice all the things my loved ones do right instead the things I perceive as wrong. In fact, there will be times when "mistakes" don't need to be mentioned at all. My loved ones are growing and learning and need room to try, fall down, and get back up without a critic looking over their shoulders. My goal for our time together is to improve on their day rather than detract from it.

15

Connection

What must you do before you leave this
earth, precious child?
Write it down. Say it. Scream it.
Whisper it. Pray it. Believe it.

WHAT'S YOUR DREAM, PRECIOUS CHILD?

I don't ask it enough.
I don't encourage it enough.
But it's brewing. It's growing roots. It's taking hold today in the hearts and minds of those standing in front of us.
"What's your dream?"

I had the chance to ask a classroom of children, one right after the other, as I signed my autograph on lined notebook paper.
There was no hesitation; they knew.
There was not one duplicate answer; they knew.

Veterinarian.
Singer.
Major league baseball player.
Reporter.
A scientist who cures cancer.
A kind person who helps others.
A chef in a fancy restaurant.
A marine biologist.

One after the other, I heard very specific dreams. I saw sparks of energy fly. I felt ripples of excitement spread. It was as if they'd been waiting to be asked.
Even my own child had dreams to voice.
But 'round here it's more like,
"Are you being nice to your sister?"
"Did you turn off the lights in your room?"
"Have you finished your homework?"

"Where are your shoes?"
But what about, "What's your dream?"
It goes sorely unspoken 'round here.
But it's not too late.
Oh no, it's not too late.

It's brewing. It's growing roots. It's taking hold right now, this very minute in the hearts and minds of the miracles standing in front of us.

Thirty-one fifth graders gently reminded me that children know what makes their hearts come alive.

It is my honor and my privilege to ask, "What's your dream, precious child?"

And then do all I can to nurture that seed to full bloom.

Today's Reminder

I rarely think about the child dreamer inside me, but she is still there. Today I will ask myself a very important question: What must you do before you leave this earth, precious child? *No matter how outlandish the answer, I will write it. I will say it. I will scream it. I will whisper it. I will pray it. I will believe it. A long time has passed since I listened to my inner dreamer, but those years have not been wasted time. Oh no. All these years and experiences have been preparing me for this moment when the child dreamer inside me can be heard and believed.*

16

Acceptance

I think the greatest gift I can give you is to
let you sigh with relief, knowing you do not
need to change today—or maybe ever.

YOU DON'T NEED TO CHANGE TODAY

I get lost easily.
I eat popcorn too quickly.
I cry at the drop of a hat.

I am too defensive about certain issues.
I need alone time each day.
I feel awkward approaching groups of people in social settings.

I am grouchy when I don't get enough sleep.
I cannot watch violent movies or graphic news clips.
I am a bit of a control freak.
I wish these things weren't so.
But they are.

For many years—decades even—I tried to change these things about myself, but I couldn't. It was useless.

I remember breathing a big sigh of relief when I finally said to myself, "You still do that thing you do. And it's not going to change today. It's okay. You're okay. Just be yourself."

That's when I got to know me. Because it was no longer necessary to note all the things I needed to "get over" or change about myself, I had the space to just be me.

I began being more understanding of my quirks, comforts, likes, and dislikes. Suddenly, I stopped seeing my "issues" as weaknesses because they are part of who I am.

And now that I'm getting to know me without conditions and reservations, I'm getting to know you, my precious child.

You like your privacy when you change clothes.

You need time—time is love to you.

You always take a moment to warm up in new situations.

Change is hard—it's better not to rush you to adapt.

The voice of understanding is the voice you hear best.

You like to lick your fingers even when there's a napkin right in front of you.

You're a friend to all and seldom get attached to one.

Long good-byes are important to you.

Now that I know you, I've adapted to these things about you, and these things don't bother me as much anymore.

Maybe you'll outgrow them.

Maybe you won't.

I think the greatest gift I can give you is to let you sigh with relief, knowing you do not need to change today—or maybe ever.

"Just be yourself," I can say, and mean it—really mean it.

Because your quirks, mannerisms, and inclinations are the texture, color, and durability that make up the beautifully unique fabric of you.

Today's Reminder

What would happen if I stopped trying to change the perceived weaknesses I see in myself and in my loved ones? What would happen if I chose to look a little deeper, take a new angle, or just wait and see? Perhaps if we were to look into each other's eyes and say, "I see you. I love you. You are exactly as God intended you to be," there would be more peace in our hearts. Today, I will stop trying to change the unchanging and cultivate peace instead.

17

Connection

"That happens to me."
Who knew such love, compassion,
understanding, and kindness could be
contained in four simple words?

THE ONE WHO NOTICES

The painfully shy waiter returned to our table with a cup that was filled to the brim. Because it had no lid, the soda spilled when he set it down. A look of distress crossed his face, and he flushed. I grabbed my napkin and was just about to say it was okay, but my child beat me to the punch, and her response was far better than mine would have been.

"That happens to me," she said, looking straight into the young man's face with a reassuring smile.

She did not say the usual, "It's okay," or "Don't worry about it."

She said, "That happens to me."

Who knew such love, compassion, understanding, and kindness could be contained in four simple words?

The waiter looked down shyly, and I detected a slight sigh of relief. When he left, my daughter said, "I'm glad he has that job. He's good at his job." Apparently a little spilled soda didn't diminish him in her eyes.

I often forget the power of compassion. Among the busyness and the hurry, honest mistakes become bigger deals than they actually are. Among the daily distractions and pressures, small blunders are treated like major catastrophes.

How easy it is to sigh with exasperation, as if my whole day is ruined by one tiny mistake that may inconvenience my life for a whole two minutes.

How easy it is to forget that I make mistakes too. But through a spilled soda and a little girl's loving response, I was reminded of how I want to live.

Let us notice each other's pain and ambivalence.
Even if we are different.
Even if we don't wear the same clothes.

Even if we don't have the same job or the same IQ.
Because in our hearts we are more alike than we are different.

Let us acknowledge each other's slip-ups and failures with compassion and grace.
Even if it does cause a mess.
Even if it takes a moment of our time.
Even if it's the last thing we feel like doing.
Because we are all just looking for someone to stand beside us in our mess.

Let us respond with patience to the mistakes of our children.
Even if we've never made such a mistake.
Even if we saw it coming.
Even if we are at our wits' end.
Because in our memory banks we can all remember standing in the school cafeteria with the eyes of judgment upon us.

Let us notice when someone is struggling to get it right, fit in, or please us.
Even if it's not perfect.
Even if their hands shake.
Even if someone else does it far better.
Because in our souls we are all hungry for acceptance.

Let us remember we are all just waiting for someone to notice—notice our pain, notice our scars, notice our fear, notice our joy, notice our triumphs, notice our courage.

And the one who notices is a rare and beautiful gift.

Today's Reminder

Nothing blocks joy from a home or a heart more than exasperation, annoyance, or shame in response to mistakes or missteps. Today I will meet my loved ones' mistakes with compassion. I will say, "That happens to me too," or "Making mistakes means we are learning and trying." Instead of fear, embarrassment, or frustration, I might see relief, hope, or determination on that face I love. I will also gain trust for larger infractions in the future.

18

Authenticity

In the face of pain and struggle, don't shut
down; stay open.
Refuse to miss the joy waiting for you today.

A Feeling Life

I don't wanna swallow apologetic words
just because it's easier than saying them.

I don't wanna light my life by the glow of the screen
just because it takes too much effort to get outside.

I don't wanna hide my real feelings
just because it's easier to fake a smile.

I don't wanna stay on the surface
just because it hurts to go deep.

I don't wanna fill my emptiness with food, work, or booze
just because it's more convenient than seeking inner peace.

I don't wanna merely exist each day of my life
just to avoid the pain that comes with feeling.

A Feeling Life takes courage, effort, struggle, and exposure—
exposure to the pain,
exposure to the uncertainty,
exposure to the hard truths.

A Feeling Life
is not always sun on my face,
is not always a belly laugh from the soul,
is not always sweet lips on my cheek.
But if I walk around blocking myself from the pain, I block
the joy.

I don't wanna miss opening my heart to the goodness
just because it's easier for it to stay closed up.
I wanna feel the sun on my face.
I wanna feel the belly laugh from my soul.
I wanna feel the sweet lips on my cheek.
I wanna feel peace within my grasp.
So I will accept the pain that comes with a Feeling Life
because I don't wanna miss the joy.

Today's Reminder

Today there is a good chance I will experience pain, struggle, challenge, sadness, frustration, or uncertainty. This does not mean I am failing. It does not mean I am going about things all wrong; it means I am alive. I refuse to numb myself to, deny, or dwell on this unpleasant feeling or experience when it comes. I will acknowledge it and remind myself it won't last forever. I refuse to merely exist. This means I will accept the pain that comes with a Feeling Life and grasp joy every chance I get.

19

Connection

A compassionate response can shed light on unfamiliar territory.

UNFAMILIAR TERRITORY

I have a terrible sense of direction. Every time I get lost, my palms sweat as I grip the steering wheel. I wonder nervously how many wrong turns I will make and how late I will be. I've learned to calm myself by remembering that although I might be lost temporarily, I always seem to find my way home.

Surprisingly, my fear of unknown territory became a positive one day. It was the day my child had to swim in a ten-lane competition pool. It was much larger and deeper than the one she was used to, and her fear showed in her face.

There was a time in my life when I would have dismissed her fears by saying, "Come on, you're being ridiculous," or "It's not that big of a deal," but I recognized that look of fear on my child's face. It was exactly how my face looks every time I get lost. Instead of dismissing her this time, I offered my child a little compassion and a little understanding. I immediately noticed that my assurances gave her more courage than any words of condemnation ever did.

My daughter bravely swam in that big, unfamiliar pool that day. And when she exited the water after her event, her beaming face said it all.

"I will remember this," I said to myself, and now I offer this reminder to us all:

Whether they're sleeping without a night-light, riding a bike without training wheels, or nervously eyeing the neighbor's dog . . .

Whether it's the first job interview, a noisy thunderstorm, or a driver's test . . .

Whether it's going to camp, trying out for the school play, or fetching something in the dark basement . . .

It's unfamiliar territory. And a fear that may seem silly or insignificant to us may be quite real to them.

So instead of dismissing their fears, remember a time when you were scared, uncertain, and worried. Perhaps by remembering, you can offer a little compassion, a little understanding, and a chance to overcome a challenge. In doing so, you may shed light on unfamiliar territory, so those who are lost can reach the other side of fear and find their way home.

Today's Reminder

Today I will not be so quick to shrug off my loved one's worry, fear, sadness, and frustration. If I pause for just a moment, I might be able to remember a time I felt that way. In my time of need, what would have helped me overcome my fear? I will offer my worried loved one what I wish had been offered to me.

20

Connection

Speak softly and gently. Do not rush them.
Just stay close
so they know you're here to help.
(Advice for those in cages both seen and unseen.)

REACHING THROUGH CAGES

For many months, my daughters and I visited a shelter for homeless cats at a local PetSmart. It quickly became one of our favorite pastimes to pet the cats through the cages, talk to them, read the stories of how they came to be there, and wish we could adopt them all.

One day we went to check on "Louie," whose description card said his beloved owner had to go into a retirement home. It was reported on the card that he'd been depressed ever since. His sad eyes had confirmed this.

When we arrived at the little cat room, we scanned the cages looking for the majestic, long-haired black cat. To our surprise, he was not there.

"Who are you looking for?" asked the woman volunteering there.

"Louie," we said.

"Louie was adopted!" she said, and smiled.

We proceeded to ask about "Cottonball," the long-haired calico who had been in the corner cage. After giving us updates, the woman handed me her card and said they could use volunteers to socialize the cats and clean their cages.

As my children rejoiced at the invitation, I had one predominant thought: *We won't have to reach through the cages!* Finally, there will be no metal bars between us and these beautiful creatures.

My daughters and I talked about our first day on the job for a solid week. I warned them that there might be animals who did not want us to touch them. We talked about the frightened cats who might try to bite or scratch when we moved things around in their cages.

It dawned on me that in some cases we would still be reaching through cage bars to connect to the beating hearts within.

My older daughter quickly piped up with a plan. "I will speak softly and gently. I will not rush him out of the cage. I will just stay close so he knows I am there to help."

Yes, I thought. *Yes!* What a beautiful approach to those (both animals and humans) who might be in cages, including the kind we cannot see:

Those who are shy.
Those who have suffered great loss.
Those who never had much to lose.

Those who have been laughed at or shunned.
Those who have been shuffled back and forth.
Those looking for a place to belong.

Those facing major battles they cannot talk about.
Those with secrets too horrible to speak.
Those having a really hard day.

Those in new situations and unfamiliar territories.
Those weighed down with decisions.
Those weighed down with no options.

For those in hindering cages we cannot see:
May we have compassion when we notice sad eyes.
May we wonder what caused pain so deep they must lash out.

May we consider how abandonment feels.
May we look past the scars, the stuttering, and the nail biting.
May we smile when others turn away.

May we speak softly and gently.
May we not rush them.
May we just stay close so they know we're here to help.

Yes. Oh yes. I think compassion might be the key to opening
the cages we cannot see.
With a soft voice,
a loving response,
or a small attempt to relate,
we can reach through the bars of cages unseen
and connect to the beating hearts within.

Today's Reminder

Today I as I go out into the world, either as someone in a cage unseen or as someone willing to reach into a cage, I will use a universal sign for belonging. I will clasp my hands together as if I'm holding my own hand. This gesture says, "I'm being brave by showing up right now. Can anyone see me?" I will look for those with sad eyes, fidgety hands, or hunched shoulders. When I see them, I will smile warmly. I do not want to miss the invitation to step fully into life and connect to the beating heart within.

21

Acceptance

Remember, every person you encounter is somebody's child.

SOMEBODY'S CHILD

The best piece of advice I ever received came from a teaching colleague when I was telling her about Grace, the Persistent Question Asker of my classroom who tested my patience daily.

"Just remember, every little person in that room is somebody's child," the veteran teacher said, with a mix of understanding and authority.

The next day when Grace arrived, I met her cheerful gaze a little longer and gave her a wide smile. Like the lyrics to an old '50s song, I kept hearing, "She's somebody's baby . . . somebody's baby." For the first time, I saw Grace as someone's most beloved gift who, for whatever reason, needed extra assurances, extra hugs, extra smiles.

That slight but significant change in my perspective made a
huge difference that resulted in
a little more patience,
a little more kindness,
a little more compassion,
a little more tolerance
for Grace.

Now, ten years later, I have children of my own and the thought of Grace helps me daily.

When my child is walking too slowly, I am reminded that her legs can't go as fast as mine.

Just because my life is dictated by the pace of an adult world doesn't mean my child's should be.

When my child takes her sweet time deciding which outfit to wear or what snack to have, I am reminded that children need time to select among an array of choices.

Just because I have learned to be decisive and often ignore the luxury of contemplation doesn't mean my child should have to.

When I want to sigh with exasperation as she pours the milk too quickly and it overflows from her cereal bowl, I am reminded that accuracy comes with practice.

Just because I get irritated with myself when I make mistakes doesn't mean my child should be subjected to the same unreasonable standards.

When she searches high and low for her misplaced shoes,
when she can't seem to focus on homework,

when she acts silly in serious situations,
when I find myself expecting perfection, speed, accuracy, and maturity from my child,
I think of Grace.
Then I look at my child, who won't be little forever, and I say to myself:
She is somebody's child.
She is my child.
She is my gift—my everyday miracle.
Let me treat her as such.

Today's Reminder

Today I will not push the growth process. I am becoming. She is becoming. He is becoming. We are becoming. It may feel like others are passing us by or getting ahead, but we will focus only on our lane. We are right where we need to be. We are developing into who we're meant to become. Such a miraculous process takes time.

22

Authenticity

I'd never want to be the reason the world
doesn't get to hear your song.

I WANT THE WORLD TO HEAR YOUR SONG

I could choose to say something about the way you look in that outfit or how you do your hair.
I could choose to say something about the order in which you do your homework or make your bed.

I could choose to say something about the way you play the G chord when you practice your guitar.
I could choose to say something about the way you laugh a little too loudly or run a little too slowly.
But I'm pretty sure you'd lose that confident stride you have marching into school.
I'm pretty sure you'd start to second-guess yourself and the way you do things.
I'm pretty sure you'd begin to worry about other people's opinions rather than letting your heart be your guide.
I'm pretty sure you wouldn't feel comfortable belting out the lyrics that come straight from your soul.
I'm pretty sure your light would dim.
I'm pretty sure your laugh would change.
So I've chosen to reserve my comments for the most important things and help *you* be the mistake finder rather than me. I've chosen to remember that just because it doesn't look "right" to me doesn't mean it's wrong.
I've noticed you're happy in that outfit you love so much. You're pleased with the way you do your hair. The way you complete your work and laugh with abandon are just fine.
I'd never want to be the reason you swallow words and keep worries to yourself.
I'd never want to be the reason you stop laughing with the joy of a contented soul.
I'd never want to be the reason the world doesn't get to hear your song.

Today's Reminder

Today I will refrain from instructing, critiquing, and managing under the guise of "good intentions." Instead, I will make it abundantly clear that I love my people "as is," meaning they do not need to do *anything,* be *anything, or* change *anything to be loved by me. I will make a point to say, "I love you just as you are, exactly as you are. I love you because you are you." Feeling known and accepted by the people in our home not only makes for a better day, but it also makes for a better future.*

23

Acceptance

Come as you are.
Let me see that light within you.
Let me tell you how beautiful it is.

COME AS YOU ARE

Come as you are.

Come with your hair uncombed.
Come with your crooked teeth.
Come with your sad eyes.

Come with your shaky confidence.
Come with your head in the clouds.
Come with the warts you hope nobody sees.

Come with your inability to sit still.
Come with your incessant questions.
Come with your fidgety hands.

Come with your outside-the-box thinking.
Come with your painfully shy smile.
Come with your voice too loud.

Come with your loneliness.
Come with your scars.
Come with the story you think nobody wants to hear.

Come with your fears.
Come with your tear-stained cheeks.
Come with your heart on your sleeve.

Come as you are.
Just come as you are.

You might think I'm doing you a favor by opening my arms to you, but that is not the case. I am the one who is about to be blessed by the not-so-obvious gifts within you—the gifts other people don't see because they fail to look past the surface.

Come as you are, I say.
Let me see that light within you.
Let me tell you how beautiful it is.

Today's Reminder

Today I want to rejuvenate myself by experiencing a moment of comfort. It's been a while, so I will think back. What made me feel happy as a child? Was it the smell of a library book? Perhaps it was the sound of crickets. Perhaps it was strumming a guitar or walking barefoot in the grass. I will go back to a happy memory when I felt accepted, content, and comfortable and try to recreate it. Perhaps I will invite someone to join me. I'll be sure to say, "Come as you are."

24

ACCEPTANCE

You deserve a day, if not one thousand more,
to be celebrated, appreciated, and lovingly
adored.

YOU DESERVE A DAY

You deserve a day to feel beautiful in your own skin,
a day when body parts are neither too fat nor too thin.

You deserve a day to see your valued presence on this earth,
a day when age, weight, and IQ don't determine your worth.

You deserve a day when you can speak your mind with ease,
a day where lifelong dreams are yours to seize.

You deserve a day where your spirit rises like a red balloon,
a day without judgment and guilt to last for many moons.

You deserve a day to feel good in the place where you are,
a day to embrace your imperfections and heal your
hidden scars.

You deserve a day to feel proud of the life you've made,
a day when regrets and past mistakes permanently fade.

You deserve a day to be loved without restraint,
a day free from being judged a sinner or a saint.

You belong in a valley with daffodils beneath your feet;
you belong in an orchard with apples, tasty and sweet.

You belong on a hammock with a cold drink in hand;
you belong in a field of sunflowers, fragrant and grand.

You belong in the sunshine but never in the rain;
you belong in a place of safety, far from misery and pain.

You belong on an island with warm breezes in your hair;
you belong in a peaceful sanctuary, free from worry and care.

You belong in a place of forgiveness and grace;
you belong with rays of hope shining on your face.

You deserve a day, if not one thousand more,
to be celebrated, appreciated, and lovingly adored.

Today's Reminder

Today I will give myself something of value that will enhance my life. An extra hour of sleep. A colorful water bottle to encourage proper hydration. A crisp new journal to write down my dreams. An hour of exercise or creativity. And if nothing else, I will give myself a moment. Everyone needs a moment of grace, forgiveness, or acceptance every now and then. I am worthy of gifts and goodness too.

25

Authenticity

Even when she wasn't getting it "right,"
it didn't mean her children were going to
turn out all wrong.

THE SILVER LINING THAT COMES WITH FALLING DOWN

She wanted to believe it wasn't too late to be kind to herself.

"But forty-two years is a long time. Old habits die hard," she thought.

She decided to try anyway.

She stopped beating herself up over past failures.

She stopped replaying mistakes over and over in her head.

She was open about her shortcomings, real with her humanness, and generous with her apologies.

"I don't always get it right, and I never will," she admitted.

This was not something to be sad about, because there was a silver lining—a major one:

Even on the days she didn't get it right, her children were still learning valuable lessons about perseverance, determination, failure, compassion, grace, and forgiveness. Even when she wasn't getting it "right," it didn't mean her children were going to turn out all wrong.

Her humanness allowed her children to be human.

Her courage to keep showing up gave her children courage to show up.

Loving herself despite her failures, flaws, and imperfections gave her children permission to love themselves "as is."

As a result, her children discovered an empowering truth much sooner than she did—that you can't see the silver lining that comes from falling down until you get back up.

Each time this woman pulled herself back up from a fall, her soul shone boldly and bravely, and her loved ones breathed a sigh of relief knowing mistakes were not the end of the world. They were a beginning, a chance to shine bravely and boldly in the light of imperfection and grace.

"Be kind to yourself," the children said to themselves and to each other.

"Only love today," she said to herself—sometimes fifty times a day. Until one day it finally sank in, and she truly believed.

Forty-two years was not too late to be kind to herself.

And it wasn't too soon for the ones she loved most.

Today's Reminder

Each time the critic in my head starts to make a hurtful comment, each time my inner bully tries to tear me down, each time the hate talker inside me tries to spew vicious lies, I will fight back with three mighty words: Only Love Today. *I will acknowledge the challenges I've endured and how I manage to show up even when it's hard, even when it's the last thing I want to do. I will see myself through the eyes of those who love me. They don't see imperfections, failings, and mistakes; they see love, never-failing love. I will try to see it too. It's not too late.*

26

Connection

"How would you do it?"
In five words, we can let our loved ones shine.

HAIRBRUSH OFFERING

"How would you do it?" I asked in a shaky voice, offering her the hairbrush.

My then four-year-old child looked shocked. This was the

last thing she expected from her grumpy manager mother. Her years of requests to brush her own hair had always been met with "Not today."

But today I couldn't take looking at that angry, impatient woman in the mirror staring back at me. And this, the hairbrush offering, felt like one small step to bring back my joy.

With small but agile hands, my daughter brushed the sides of her hair from top to bottom until the hair was silky smooth. She then carefully draped her hair softly over her shoulders and smiled proudly at her reflection. The manager in me noticed she did not brush the back of her head, but I remained quiet.

My child met my eyes in the mirror. "Thank you, Mama! I always wanted to do that."

With those words, I felt as though I'd been given a gift. I vowed to look for more potential hairbrush offerings to reduce the managing and increase the nurturing in my interactions with my loved ones. It didn't take long to see there were many opportunities to open my hands and ask, *How would you do it?*

The ways my spouse took care of the children, tidied his area of the bedroom, prepared meals, put away the groceries, and paid the bills were not wrong—just different from the ways I do things.

The ways my older daughter packed her swim team bag, emptied her swim team bag, saved money, selected gifts, completed projects, did homework, and baked cookies were not wrong—just different from the ways I do things.

The way the chatty clerk bagged my groceries, the way my colleague took ten extra steps to accomplish a task, the way my sister sipped coffee and read the paper before starting our day together were not wrong—just different from the ways I do things.

How would you do it?

Those five words became an olive branch in times of conflict.

Those five words acted as a springboard, propelling my loved ones to new heights.

Those five words brought peace to my home and heart.

Try a hairbrush offering today. As the blessings unfold in your open hands, don't be surprised if a long-lost smile returns to your face.

Today's Reminder

By responding with more compassion, patience, and acceptance, I will begin to see less in black and white and more in color. What I think needs changing may not need changing at all. When I stop correcting long enough to listen, love, and be inspired by the uniqueness of my loved ones, I will see colors I don't have but wish I did. Today I'll step back and let them be who they are. Perhaps it will be their long-awaited moment to shine.

27

Acceptance

By listening, validating, supporting, and
inviting you to just be yourself,
you can simply be a kid—a kid I so
dearly love.

I'LL GIVE IT BACK TO YOU

"Figure out what you're going to do with your life," they say.
Maybe she's just trying to figure out how to get through
today.

"Figure out how to perfect that swing," they say.
Maybe he's just trying to figure out where he belongs.

"Figure out how you can get that grade up," they say.
Maybe she's just trying to figure out how to reach out
for help.

"Figure out how you can get recognized for your talent,"
they say.
Maybe he's just trying to recognize his own worth.

"Figure out how you can excel," they say.
Maybe she's just figuring out how to make a true friend,
or find her dignity,
or quiet the critical voice in her head.

I realize I put too much pressure on you, my precious child. I just want what's best for you—but sometimes my hopes and concerns come out too controlling, too negative, and too strong. I often forget you have your own set of worries, struggles, and challenges to try to cope with each day.

Pressure is already abundant in your young life. It's in the music you listen to; it's in the shows you watch; it's in the hallways and in the classrooms; it's on the field, in the stands, and on the stage; it's in your conversations, your friendships, and your conflicts. Pressure is in your head and in your heart. And there you are, just trying to be a kid and enjoy this childhood of yours (which doesn't always feel like yours).

I can give it back to you—a little of it, at least. Today we'll go to the frozen yogurt shop and figure out the best flavor combination. I'll sit across from you so you can see the love shining in my eyes. I'll tell you how proud I am to be your parent. I'll tell you that you don't have to *do* anything or *be* anything other than who you are. I'll tell you I love you just as you are, exactly as you are.

I hope these minutes we spend not figuring out the heavy stuff will make room for laughter and light to come in. I hope it'll be the beginning of more moments wherein your heart and mind can just be a kid.

I don't want to add to the pressure—there's enough of that in your world.

I want you to enjoy this childhood of yours.

After all, it's precious, and it's fleeting.

So I'll try to give it back to you whenever I can by listening, validating, supporting, and inviting you to just be yourself—a kid I so dearly love.

Today's Reminder

Today the motto of the day is "Breathing Room." Let there be breathing room when it comes to the field goals my loved ones miss, the messes on their bedroom floor, or the way they got dressed. Let there be breathing room when it comes to their daily schedules and the pressure on their shoulders. Let there be breathing room when it comes to their emotions, fears, and doubts. Taking risks, learning, growing, and expressing emotion mean there will be mistakes; there will be meltdowns; there will be challenges. I will give my people breathing room to be human so their spirits have oxygen to prosper and thrive.

28

Acceptance

If you look a little deeper and gaze a little longer, you'll see all that I am.

WHAT YOUR BELOVED WANTS YOU TO SEE

Just for today, look beyond the flaws, the whines, the protests. Look beyond the stain on the front of my new white shirt.

Just for today, look beyond the spills, the unbrushed teeth,
the absent-mindedness.
Look beyond the missed spelling words, the ones we
practiced together last night.

Just for today, look beyond the ill-fitting pants and the
rocks you find in my pocket.
Look beyond the fact that I am impossible to put to bed.

Just for today, look beyond the daydreamer,
the dawdler,
the messy artist,
the introvert,
the Energizer Bunny that keeps going and going.
Just for today, look beyond and see.
See me for what I am: a child who has many needs but also
has a heart full of love.
See that beneath the dirt-stained pants and pouty lip, I am
your everyday miracle.
Your everyday miracle.
If you look a little deeper and gaze a little longer, you'll see
all that I am.

Today's Reminder

Today I will make an effort to see the positives in my loved ones. Perhaps I will notice how my child makes the bed and arranges the stuffed animals in a certain way. I might notice how my beloved never fails to greet me with a smile. I may notice the way my child encouraged a teammate during the game. When we have a quiet moment, I will say, "I noticed something special about you," and then I will describe what I saw. Seeing the good in someone is a powerful motivator, but there is something more. Highlighting a special talent or gift I see in my loved one might lead him or her to take a risk, go after a lifelong goal, or try an unexpected career path. By shifting my focus from what my loved ones can't *do to what they* can *do, a whole new world might open up.*

29

Connection

You are worth consideration of the most gentle, loving kind.

CONSIDER SAVING SOMETHING OF VALUE

You see crooked teeth and an overbite.
I see someone who invites people in with her smile.

You see obtrusive eyewear.
I see bright, kind eyes behind the lenses.

You see two left feet on the dance floor.
I see someone who knows how to have fun and not take life too seriously.

You see deep lines between your eyebrows.
I see years of nurturing, caring, living, and loving.

You see extra padding pulling against your shirt.
I see the way you embrace others with your whole heart.

You see ugly, red acne.
I see a young person with clever ideas, articulate words, and a beautiful future.

You see a failure.
I see someone who has pulled herself up more times than
I can count.

You see age spots.
I see a hand I'd like to hold when I need strength and guidance.

You see a divorcée.
I see resilience.

You see a defect.
I see strength.

You see a victim.
I see a survivor.

When you look in the mirror or at a picture of yourself, perhaps you are quick to judge, critique, and beat down.

Today, I ask you to do something different. Today, I ask you to consider.

Consider the best possible perspective of your flaws and imperfections. Consider the possibility that you might be the only one who even sees them.

Consider the possibility that your story, your personality, or your contribution to the world outshines your flaws and imperfections. Consider the importance of your presence to those around you.

Today, would you consider seeing the goodness others see when they look at you?

By considering, instead of criticizing, something valuable might be saved.

Your smile,
your laugh,

your words,
your song,
your ideas,
your dance moves,
your jokes,
your wisdom
are hindered each time you see the worst, instead of the best, in yourself.

Dear one, you are worth consideration of the most gentle, loving kind.
Today, would you consider your value?
I can assure you, others do.
And we cannot, for one minute, imagine life without what you bring to it.

Today's Reminder

Rather than saving "I love you" during nighttime tuck-in, departure time, holiday, or celebration, I vow to get into the habit of saying it when I feel it—such as when her beauty astounds me; when his giving heart shines through; when I notice the joy my beloved people bring to the world. When the words "I love you" are not tied to situations or achievements, they are better emphasized, better heard, and better absorbed by my loved one's ears and heart.

30

Connection

I hope after spending an hour, a day, a lifetime in my presence,
I leave your heart fuller,
your smile wider,

your spirit stronger,
your future brighter
than you could have ever imagined by yourself.

PRESENCE PLEDGE

I hope you feel like a welcome spark in my life, not an inconvenience, annoyance, or bother to my day.

I hope you feel comfortable in your skin, not constantly wondering how many things you need to change before you're unconditionally loved and celebrated.

I hope you feel heard, valued, and understood, not dismissed for being too young and too inexperienced to have an opinion or know what you need to thrive.

I hope you feel capable and confident, not fearful or incapable of doing something without constant supervision and correction.

I hope you feel brave enough to bare the colors of your soul, not pressured to hide your light or play small to gain acceptance.

I hope after spending an hour, a day, a lifetime in my presence,
I leave your heart fuller,
your smile wider,
your spirit stronger,
your future brighter,
than you could have ever imagined by yourself.

Today's Reminder

Today I will surrender my need to be right or teach a lesson and instead make meaningful connection my sole desire. I will ask my loved ones how I can support them and then listen—just listen. Instead of trying to fix the problem or dictate the next move, I will simply ask, "How can I best support you?" or "How can I help?" These two questions bring down defenses, validate feelings, and put us on the same team. It will be empowering for my loved ones to know I am for them, not against them. I will try to support them in a way that allows them to feel heard and respected.

31

AUTHENTICITY

Letting go of "perfect" brings freedom,
peace, love, and acceptance to ourselves and
to those who follow in our footsteps.

LETTING GO OF PERFECT

Never will I forget the days when I thought tasks had to be accomplished with 100 percent accuracy or they might as well not be done at all.

Never will I forget how a whole day could be ruined when one little thing on my master plan went awry.

Never will I forget when school projects had to be flawless, when kitchen counters had to be spotless, when the drive to get "one more thing" accomplished was endless.

Sadly, I might still be living such an existence today had it not been for the impact this approach to life was having on my children. You see, all that pressure to be perfect couldn't be contained inside my own lines. It often had the tendency to spill out and contaminate my children's day, their perspective, their spirit, and their joy.

When I realized the underlying message my children were hearing, absorbing, and internalizing was, "You're not good enough," I vowed to change. Little by little, I started to let go of the pursuit of perfection. I began to let things *be* as they were and stopped trying to control everything. I found myself saying things such as:

It was just an accident—it can be cleaned up.

Tell me your opinion. I like to hear what you think.

I love the person you are—exactly as you are.

How would you do it? Show me.

Now when I see my children embracing mismatched socks and do-it-yourself ponytails,

transforming mistakes on their paper into hearts,

taking risks even though they may not succeed,

and saying, "Everybody makes mistakes,"

I take it as confirmation of the way I want to live.

Letting go of "perfect" brings freedom, peace, love, and acceptance to ourselves and to those who follow in our footsteps.

Today's Reminder

Today I take one step toward "letting go of perfect" by periodically asking myself these questions: What am I telling myself needs to be done today? What am I saying to myself about my parenting skills? My job performance? My appearance? Today I will have realistic standards. I will lower the bar. I will let go of something that is not necessary. I will ban the word should *from my vocabulary. When I close my eyes tonight, I will ask myself,* Did I show up? *If the answer is yes, that is enough. Love doesn't have to be perfect (or anywhere near it) to be cherished, appreciated, and remembered.*

32

Acceptance

Be softer today.
Let love begin to smooth away the rough edges.

THE GIFT OF ACCEPTANCE

Throughout the first ten years of our marriage, I often thought about the things I wanted to change in my husband. I wished he would open up more. I wished he would listen better. I wished he would notice when things needed to be picked up around the house, look me in the eyes when we talked, and chew his gum quietly. I really wished he wouldn't make such a fuss when it came to birthdays and holidays. (How dare he?)

I spent a lot of time wishing my husband would be someone different.

One day, the two of us were having a heated moment. Before any new experience I tend to get very anxious and worried. My husband was telling me to relax. I said, "This is a new experience for me! I get anxious. Haven't you figured this out yet? This is who I am. I am not going to change. And it's okay. Maybe it doesn't need to be changed."

Oh.

While I was standing there wanting him to see me, love me, "as is," I saw him for who he was.

When I decided to stop wishing for him to change, I noticed he opened up at night when the lights were out and he was my focus. I noticed he listened carefully when I said, "This is important." I noticed he took care of many things around the house that were never on my radar. I realized he wasn't trying to outdo me on gifting; he just loved to give and had a knack for remembering exactly what people like. When he chewed gum loudly, I reminded myself I would miss the sound of it someday. The sound became (almost) comforting.

The best gift I ever gave my husband was acceptance, and it turned out to be a gift to me as well.

If you are wondering where to start the process of offering acceptance—whether to your spouse, your child, or yourself—start by contemplating the type of love you wish to receive. By defining and envisioning the love you hope for, there's a likelihood you will begin to embody it and thus offer it. Let this definition get you started:

Let me be love.

Not the shiny, perfectly worded, flashy and flowery love
that comes and goes with special occasions or when
it's convenient.

Let me be the messy, genuine, put in the effort, feel it in
your bones, come as you are, kind of love.

Let me be the Show Up kind of love that is found where it is
least expected and when it is most needed.

Let me be the mountain-moving type of love that offers
hope and makes growth possible.

Let me be the kind of love that silences hate talk, breaks
down barriers, and cannot be contained by chains
or cages.

Let me be the unconditional, limitless love that rises with the sun and stretches beyond annoying quirks, bad habits, and human failings.

Let me be the wholly accepting love that makes for a soft place to lay one's head at night—for both the giver and the receiver.

Let me be love.

Today's Reminder

What kind of love do I want to be today? I will write it down. By declaring my heart's hope, I get one step closer to bringing it to life. I will think about that hope when I encounter something I want to change or critique in my loved one. Before I speak, I will say to myself, Let me be love. *Perhaps I'll realize this is not the time to mention change. If I still feel as though I need to address it later, I will do so with kindness. Who knows? Maybe I'll realize change is not needed. Maybe I'll realize he is fine the way he is. Perhaps I'll realize her way is perfectly acceptable. Maybe what I will see is an opportunity to give my loved one the gift of acceptance, a powerful act of love with the potential to come back to me.*

33

Authenticity

Despite the marred pages of my past,
today is a blank page
lined with yesterday's wisdoms and braveries,
making me more compassionate to others
and stronger for myself.

TODAY IS A BLANK PAGE

Sometimes I look back on my life and want to delete that day,
that stupid mistake,
that rash decision,
that agonizing seventy-two-hour period,
that blow-up,
that breakdown,
that embarrassing infraction,
that careless slip of the tongue.
I want to delete them from my life as if they never happened.
Because regret hurts, shame burns, remorse sticks.
But then I have a heart-to-heart with my almost-teenage daughter,
I have an honest dialogue with a friend,
I have a little talk with myself,
and I realize something.
If I were to delete my most regretful experiences,
I wouldn't be here, on this particular page, in the story of my life.
I wouldn't have the wisdom that allows me to look in my child's eyes and say, "I know how it feels to never want to show your face again. I survived, and I know you will too."
I wouldn't have the compassion to hold my friend's hand and say, "That happened to me too. You are not alone."
I wouldn't have the experience that causes me to stop and think before making the same mistake twice.
If I deleted all the poor choices, the pitfalls, and the wrong turns of my life,
my story would not be what it is today; I would not be who I am.
But here's the best part:

despite the marred pages of my past,
today is a blank page
lined with yesterday's wisdoms and braveries
that came from falling down and getting back up.
My story is not pretty; it's flawed, but it's real, and it's still going.
Lately I've noticed a beautiful theme emerging:
Hope renews. Self-compassion heals. Forgiveness frees.
Today is a blank page. I will hold on to the hope that with each page, my story only gets better.

Today's Reminder

Today I will release a heavy burden. I will voice what feels unspeakable to a trusted soul. I might start with: "I need help," "I am afraid." "I am overwhelmed," or "I haven't felt like myself in a while." There is something about voicing the burden that makes it feel lighter, and this is why: when we meet each other in the light of realness (a place where we can love each other even more *because of our shared struggles and human imperfections), hope grows for both of us.*

34

Acceptance

Every day you speak up for the ones you love.
Today, why not speak up for yourself?

HOW TO BE YOUR OWN ADVOCATE

Come here.
Sit down for a while.
Take a load off. You work so hard.

Come here.
Tell me what's troubling you.
Your burdens are heavy. Let me bear the weight.

Come here.
Share your story.
I'll listen. There'll be no judgment from me.

Come here.
Let me hold your hand.
I know you are scared. You don't have to be strong with me.

Come here.
Lie down beside me.
Let's shut out the world out for a while.

Just for a moment, imagine putting your arm around yourself as you would a friend.
Imagine offering yourself an outstretched hand as you would someone in need.
Imagine dusting yourself off as you would a child who's fallen down.
Imagine taking a moment to encourage yourself as you would a weary colleague.

Hear that?
That's what it sounds like to be your own advocate.

By being your own advocate, you give a voice to the pain.
By being your own advocate, you drown out the critical voice and release some pressure.
By being your own advocate, you make peace with the past and expand the future.

By being your own advocate, you look after yourself. You place value on your life. You acknowledge and affirm your importance in the world.

By being your own advocate, you provide the message you needed to hear yesterday but you can still say now; it's not too late.

For just a few minutes, refrain from pushing yourself away and sit with yourself awhile. Just sit with yourself and remember you're human.

Every day you speak up for the ones you love.
Today, why not speak up for yourself?

Come here.
It's been awhile since we talked, but I haven't forgotten you.
You are loved.
You are loved.

That's the sound of being your own advocate.

It might be the message you needed to hear yesterday, but it is not too late to hear it today.

Today's Reminder

Today I will acknowledge myself. I have feelings; they are worth listening to and acknowledging. I have limits; they are necessary to keep in place as a means of valuing my time and honoring my health. I have dreams; I am worthy of time to pursue what makes my heart come alive. I have needs; I deserve affection, rest, sustenance, and grace just as everyone else does. It is not selfish to look after myself; it is critical for my happiness and well-being.

35

ACCEPTANCE

When I stopped trying to change you, you changed me.

NOW I SEE YOU

I am coming to know you—
we operate differently.
It's maddening at times
how different we are.

For so long I wanted to change parts of you:
speed you up,
rev up your ambition,
downplay your daydreams,
squelch your need to notice every little thing,
increase your efficiency,
turn up your inner drive and tone down the freedom of
your spirit.

To be honest, I tried to change the unchanging—
the beautiful wiring,
the unique fiber that makes you, *you*.
Something told me to stop—
surrender
let you *be*,
love you "as is."
And when I stopped trying to change you, you changed me.
I am more patient.
I see the emotion.

I see the colors.
I don't walk past the suffering.
I notice the tiny bugs and the giant blue sky
because you taught me to slow down, to notice and see—
  really *see*—life.
When I stopped trying to change you, you changed me
for the better.
Now I see you.
You are just right.

Today's Reminder

Today I will make one effort to embrace—or at least respect—my loved one's unique approach to life. I will remind myself he is in the process of becoming; she is in the process of finding her way. They are more apt to blossom into who they are meant to be if I stop dictating their thoughts, actions, dreams, and decisions. In the process of letting them blossom, I might do a little blossoming myself.

36

Connection

Sometimes just knowing there's a pair of
protective hands around our inner light
is all we need to carry on.

BE A LIGHT PROTECTOR

It was still early in our relationship when my then-boyfriend (now my husband) asked me to accompany him to a job interview two hours away from our college. Why would a confident guy with so many positive attributes want me to drive with him to his job interview? I was skeptical.

In my delay to respond, he must have sensed the need to explain. What he said shocked me.

"I believe in myself when you're with me. You make me stronger."

I thought back to a few times we'd studied together and how, as a budding teacher, I was always positive and encouraging. I thought about the things he said he was nervous about, including his biggest worry—that he'd have trouble getting a job. Although he was extremely bright and personable, the voice of doubt can be loud in times of uncertainty—even for the strongest people.

I went with him to that job interview. I can't even remember if he got the job. I remember only the gratitude on his face when he dropped me off afterward, saying he would've been much more nervous if he'd gone alone. All I'd done was remind him of his best qualities and encourage him to just be himself.

Over the years, I've referred to that experience many times—as a special education teacher looking into the eyes of a student who'd accidentally killed his pet, as a mother whose child admitted she felt "different" from the rest, as a confidante whose friend confessed dark truths she thought made her unworthy of love and happiness.

"You might not be able to see it right now, but you hold great value," I'd said to all of them. "I see your value. And I am here to remind you when you forget."

Perhaps today finds you watching someone you love face uncertainty, struggle, pain, or insecurity. You cannot remove it, fix it, or take it away, but you can remind them of their worth.

You can say, "I see your beautiful gifts within. I see your value. I am *for* you. You are not alone."

Sometimes all we need to believe in ourselves is one person to believe in us.

Sometimes all we need to remember our worth is to have someone point it out.

Sometimes just knowing there's a pair of protective hands around our inner light is all we need to carry on.

Today's Reminder

Today I will be a light seeker and a light protector. I will remind people of the beautiful things they know but tend to forget about themselves. Sometimes just knowing someone has protective hands around your inner light makes it stronger than what's threatening to diminish it.

37

Acceptance

Love is a good place to start a new beginning.

BUILDING ON LOVE

I wear a worn wristband that bears the words *Only Love Today*. Recently, someone asked me what that phrase meant. Although it began as a mantra to silence to my inner bully, it has become so much more.

Only Love Today means . . .

loving yourself right where you are, not when you lose some weight, not when you accomplish this or that, not when you get your life straightened out.

It means loving yourself "as is" and offering that same unconditional love to the ones who share your life.

Only Love Today means . . .

looking at your child in her mess and mayhem and remembering she's just a child who learns through her mistakes.

It means looking at yourself in your mess and mayhem and

remembering you are human—capable of mistakes and worthy of grace, just like your loved ones.

Only Love Today means . . .

recognizing the effort it takes to show up on trying days and realizing that you show up. You show up. Even when it's hard, even when you're exhausted, even when it would be easier to quit.

It means remembering your presence—your mere presence—makes someone else's day better.

Only Love Today means . . .

speaking words of kindness and compassion to yourself even when they're not the first words that come to mind.

It means adopting a positive inner dialogue so those loving words will spill out and become the inner voice of those who share your life.

Only Love Today means . . .

choosing love when it's so easy to choose criticism, judgment, ridicule, and revenge;

choosing love when it's not convenient, comfortable, or reciprocal;

choosing love when it feels as though there is no love to give;

choosing love because love is a good place to start a new beginning.

Today's Reminder

Seeing my own worth can be difficult, but noticing one positive attribute or characteristic about myself is possible. From that starting point, I can build. Today I will write something I like or love about myself on a sticky note. I will post it inside the door of a kitchen or bathroom cabinet I open frequently. I will write down another positive quality about myself the next day and every day after that until I have a significant collection of positive notes posted in the designated area. Even more, I will have awakened a love for myself I thought was long gone. I will build on that.

— III —

Fall: Wrapping In

Gratitude, Grace, and Awareness

Seeing the warm blanket in a dismal situation changes heartache to "Hallelujah, I am alive."

My teeth chatter when I feel sick and when I'm scared. I discovered this at age forty-three when I had two kidney surgeries at two different hospitals in the span of one month.

My noisy teeth got the nurse's attention as I lay there, awaiting my first surgery.

"Oh honey," she said with concern, "we need to get you a warm blanket."

She walked off briskly and came back with a pristine white blanket that had been warmed to the perfect temperature. I could not believe it. It was such an unexpected kindness, an absolute luxury, a going-the-extra-mile action I didn't think happened anymore. My teeth stopped chattering almost instantly.

"Thank you. Thank you," I said, grateful for this protective covering that I could hold on to both figuratively and literally in my time of fear.

I ended up asking for warm blankets more than pain meds during my hospital stay. I was absolutely certain they had healing powers.

As I packed my bag for my second surgery a few weeks later, I was even more nervous than the first time. I knew the sterile chill of the operating room, the count of the anesthesiologist, and the feeling of obtrusive tubes where they didn't belong.

"But don't forget the warm blankets," a little voice of hope piped up inside me.

Thank you, God, for reminding me to look forward to the warm blanket, I prayed.

The next day, I'd barely donned the surgical gown and head covering when my teeth began to chatter.

"Are you cold?" the nurse asked. I suspected it was nerves, but I nodded anyway. She pulled out this inflatable, space-age covering and showed me how to turn it on for warmth.

"Is that better?" she asked, covering my legs with what appeared to be giant Bubble Wrap.

"Yes," I lied, forcing myself to smile.

I turned to my husband in the chair next to me and whispered that it wasn't the same as a warm blanket. Scott reminded me we were in a much bigger hospital than the first, and they probably couldn't launder so many blankets.

"This is more earth-friendly anyway," he said casually, as if logical reasoning would put my complaint to rest.

It didn't. My eyes welled with tears. I excused myself and went to the bathroom. Honestly, I didn't want anyone to see me acting this way about a silly blanket. To me it wasn't silly—those blankets had been the one bright spot during a difficult time, and I'd been counting on them to comfort me in ways I could not explain.

I made it through the surgery without any warm blankets that day and actually forgot about them until my doorbell rang a few days later. As luck would have it, Scott was out running an errand and the girls were at camp. I carefully pulled myself up and slowly shuffled to the door. My neighbor stood there with a grocery bag of rotisserie chicken, a few sides, some yeast rolls, and chocolate brownies.

"It's nothing fancy, but I thought you could use a meal," she said quietly.

Before I even knew what was happening, tears of gratitude began running down my face. I hadn't lived in the neighborhood long, and hadn't told many people what I was going through, yet here was this kind woman bearing food and a look of loving concern. When she wrapped her arms around me, I thought, *Here it is! Here is my warm blanket!*

My blanket of comfort in this dismal situation had not been forgotten; it just arrived in a different form than I expected. As soon as my neighbor left, I scribbled the words "warm blanket" on a loose piece of paper in my writing folder. I found myself pausing to read that comforting phrase whenever I filed through my papers. *But what does it mean?* I wondered each time my hand touched the note. I prayed that in time, I would know.

Over the next several months, I experienced a persistent internal pain. I was examined by a nurse practitioner, two gynecologists, and three urologists. "We don't see anything abnormal," was the consensus each time. Finally, one of the doctors ordered a kidney ultrasound. I felt hopeful we'd finally have an answer, but waiting for the test results was agonizing.

"Tomorrow you go to the doctor, Mama," Natalie said one morning as I looked at the medical appointment starred on my paper calendar. "What's he going to say?" she asked as she leaned up against me so our sides touched.

"Well, he'll tell me the results of my test, and then we'll go from there," I said, not really knowing what else to tell her.

"I know what we can do," she said suddenly. "Let's make your famous sugar cookies!"

I wasn't sure where the idea came from, and I wasn't too hip about the mess we were about to make, but I felt strongly that I should say yes.

I pulled out my trusty *Better Homes and Gardens New Cook Book*, given to me by my mom when I got married. I opened right to the sugar-cookie recipe. It was the page hardened by spills and dusted with flour. The mere sight of this lovingly used page brought back fond memories and calmed my anxious soul.

When Avery heard us getting out the electric mixer, she came to help. Pretty soon we were rolling dough side by side as we had when the girls were little.

I was struck by how self-sufficient my children had become. I stood back for a moment and quietly observed my daughters, noticing how they could flatten the dough without assistance, their swimmer arms now longer and stronger than ever before. They could easily reach the counter without stools and used great restraint when shaking the colored sprinkles. There was no squabbling over the rolling pin or food coloring bottles. My ears delighted in the sound of laughter and finger licking.

I gave no regard to the flour on the kitchen floor, the fresh blue stain on the dish towel, or the medical bills lying on the kitchen counter. The clock overhead was merely a decoration, rather than a dictator of our thoughts and actions. My eyes and heart were focused on the right now, and it was all-encompassing.

Suddenly, I was overcome with gratitude. I was thankful to be alive to witness this moment—a moment that revealed just how much we'd all grown and how much we had to be grateful for.

Warm blanket.

Those words I'd scribbled on a piece of paper months earlier suddenly flashed in my head like a neon sign. Right there in the sanctity of our kitchen, we were wrapped in a warm blanket of the most divine kind—the kind that evokes deep gratitude, enabling a person to see glimmers of goodness she couldn't see before.

I'd convinced myself that those hospital blankets had healing powers; now I could see they had perspective-changing powers too.

Seeing the warm blanket in the midst of a dismal situation . . .

changed the view,

changed the air I breathed,

changed the complaints that came out of my mouth,

changed the way I spoke and responded to my loved ones and myself,

changed what was wrong to what was right.

Although I'd desperately wanted my health struggle to end so I could get on with my life, there was goodness right there in that period of uncertainty and pain. That morning, it had been tempting to allow fear, worry, pain, and doubt to take me down a negative path. It would have been easy to say no to my child, considering what I was going through at the time. But with one solitary yes, the course of my morning and my outlook improved in immeasurable ways.

From that experience, I learned that gratitude is the best way to start my day. It has the power to carry me through the rough patches and prepare my heart to love. Before I get out of bed, I say a simple prayer of thanks: "Dear God, I'm grateful to be breathing. I'm grateful for this cozy bed. I'm grateful for the people inside this house. I'm grateful for this day." The warm blanket of gratitude then drapes itself across my shoulders as I make my way down to the kitchen. When I see the shoes of my beloveds, gratitude whispers, "The people who wear those shoes love you very much. Love them well before they walk out the door. Love them well when you are reunited later today." Even though loving my people and myself is not always easy, I feel grateful for the opportunity to try. I feel grateful for another chance to love well.

As I go through the rest of my day, I keep looking for the warm blanket. It might be an understanding face, a hand squeeze, a bluebird in my yard, a favorite song, a little extra time, or an "I love you" from a family member. Once I find my warm blanket, I carry it with me, noticing the way that one warm blanket enhances my interactions, my attitude, and my day.

My friend, seeing the warm blanket in a dismal situation is a moment changer, a day changer, a life changer.

It changes the oxygen you breathe.

It changes the choices you make.

It changes annoying habits to lovable quirks.

It changes inconveniences to invitations.

It changes judgment to mercy.

It changes heartache to "*Hallelujah, I am alive.*"

There is goodness right where you are. If you can't see it yet, keep reading. In the pages ahead, I offer a collection of warm blankets that I hope will inspire greater awareness and daily grace through the power of gratitude. When wrapped in this comforting shield, life looks different. Life feels different. Life sounds different. Why? Because within the warm blanket, gratitude is abundant. And when the voice of gratitude speaks, compassion is heard. When the eyes of gratitude see, glimmers of goodness are spotted. When the touch of gratitude is felt, it has the power to change the course of your day and possibly the course of your life.

It is time to capture this perspective-altering type of gratitude that often eludes us. I say "capture" because I believe gratitude doesn't find us; we find it. And the first place we should look is within the warm blanket. Come on, crawl inside. There's plenty of room for you here, and there is much goodness to be found.

1

Gratitude

Gratitude cannot find me, but I can find it.

If I Hold My Hand There

Sometimes when I am making the bed after you've gone,
I can still feel your warmth.
And if I hold my hand there for just a moment,
this action has the power to
change my attitude,

alter my perspective,
soften my heart about
bed making,
bath giving,
food prepping,
stain removing,
car shuttling,
bill paying,
peace keeping,
and other monotonous tasks
that consume the minutes of my one precious life.
That warm spot where you peacefully slept
is my reminder
that gratitude won't find me,
but I can find it,
even among tangled sheets and strewn pajama pants,
if I rest my hand there long enough to feel it.
For one brief moment, I forget I am making a bed
and I remember instead that it is me
who gets to feel your warmth
each and every day,
even when you are away.
That's when I find gratitude
changing my perspective
on my one precious life
and what makes it so precious.

Today's Reminder

Today I will start an "I captured gratitude when . . ." list. I will keep a notepad handy in my purse, pocket, or on my bedside table so I can jot down places and experiences that make me feel grateful. By tracking my moments of gratitude like a detective, I will be more apt to notice the positives in my life. This newfound awareness will inspire a perpetual feeling of optimism and hope. I may invite my spouse, child, friend, or parent to join me in this life-changing process. I will mark the date beside each entry. This little notebook could serve as a time machine in my later years or as a way of leaving a legacy of gratitude after I am gone.

2

Grace

It won't be a perfect journey by any means,
and I surely won't get there overnight,
but this time, I like where I am heading.

HOP OFF

Funny how one battle can take the day in a negative direction.
Funny how one letdown can divert you from your true path.
Funny how one solitary criticism can take your focus off the big picture.
Funny how one slump can last and last and last.
Funny how one rejection can bleed into other areas of your life.
Funny how one poor choice can freeze you in your tracks.
Sometimes you can tell where you're heading before you even get there—and the destination is less than desirable.
This train is bound for an argument.
This train is bound for a blow-up.
This train is bound for a breakdown.
This train is bound for disconnection.
This train is bound for bitterness.

This train is bound for resentment.

I've been on that train. For two miserable years I rode it with arms crossed. I failed to realize the train stopped every once in a while, and I could hop off and change the direction I was heading.

I could hop off.

So I did.

I stopped at *Ask for Help* instead of futilely heading toward Try to Do It All.

I stopped at Only Love Today instead of pointlessly heading toward *Let Your Inner Critic Tear You Down.*

I stopped at Lower the Bar instead of tragically heading toward *Perfection at Any Cost.*

I stopped at *Forgiveness and Grace* instead of uselessly heading toward *Bitterness and Grudge-Holding Where Nobody Wins.*

Funny how I ended up in a better place when I hopped off that train going to those less-than-desirable destinations.

This train is bound for peace.

This train is bound for compassion.

This train is bound for authenticity.

This train is bound for connection.

This train is bound for reconciliation.

This train is bound for love.

It won't be a perfect journey by any means,
and I surely won't get there overnight,
but this time, I like where I am heading.

Today's Reminder

Where am I heading today? If it appears I am heading in a less-than-desirable direction, I will do whatever I can to hop off. I will call a friend. Bow my head in prayer. Say, "I'm sorry; can we begin again?" I will let go; I will forgive; I will move on. I will step outside and feel the sun on my face. I will do something for someone else. I will consider how far I've come, and where I want to go. Today I will hop off the train, leaving my baggage behind. Today I will live. This is my stop at A Better Life.

3

Awareness

That red leaf is so much more than an ordinary leaf;
it is a day in my life, and quantities are limited.

THANK YOU, RED LEAF

As I walked past my bedroom window, I saw a vibrant red leaf drifting down, down, down.
It stopped me in the middle of my daily grind.
This vibrant red leaf stopped me cold.

I watched that red leaf settle on the dead grass—
that beautiful red leaf I would trample with my boots on any ordinary Tuesday,
that beautiful red leaf I would stuff into a plastic bag with a gloved hand on any ordinary Saturday.

But not today.

Despite the duties and the deadlines, I went outside and picked up that red leaf.
I thought about pinning it to my shirt as a reminder,
but I didn't need to.
That red leaf got its point across.

That red leaf is so much more than an ordinary leaf;
it is a day in my life,
and quantities are limited.

Whether it be a frantic Monday or a draining Wednesday,
each day is a leaf drifting down, down, down.
It might not be a vibrant, red leaf that takes my breath away,
but it's a leaf that will never be on my tree of life again.

So today I've decided to look for the reds, the yellows,
and even the crispy browns
in this particular leaf of my life.
I will see it in the toothless smiles,
in the missed field goals,
in the noisy dinnertime commotion,
in the homework that brings eraser marks and tears,
and in the sticky fingers that leave me smelling like
pancake syrup.

Thank you, red leaf,
for reminding me not to walk past so quickly
or discard you with the trash
without noticing how truly miraculous you are,
even on your worst day.

Today's Reminder

Today I will look for the red leaf in my day; and no matter how tiny, or how fleeting, or how imperfect it is, I will celebrate it. I will choose to focus on what's going right instead of what's going wrong. I choose to embrace today for what it is: a brand-new chance to love and be loved. Even the briefest moment of loving connection has the potential to carry me through a rough patch.

4

Gratitude

The best days of life are not defined by grand occasions or money spent—but instead by being in the company of someone who loves us.

BECAUSE OF YOU

Thank you for the early wake-ups.
Because of you, I will never sleep away my life.

Thank you for the bedtime troubles.
Because of you, I will always know how it feels to be needed.

Thank you for your sweaty hand in mine.
Because of you, I will always know what it feels like to hold on to life.

Thank you for taking your sweet time.
Because of you, I will never rush through all the best parts.

Thank you for making me laugh until I cry.
Because of you, I will always know how to feel young at heart.

Thank you for counting on me.
Because of you, I will always know that giving up is not an option.

Because of you, I will always have
someone who comes to my arms for comfort,

someone who grants unlimited do-overs,
someone who never runs out of kisses,
someone who reminds me that the best days are not defined by grand occasions or money spent, but simply by the fact that I am in the company of someone who loves me.

Today's Reminder

When the needs of my loved ones begin to drain me, I will give thanks for the very important role I play in their lives. Yes, the people I care about can be exhausting and even maddening at times, but I get to love them. I get to hold them. I get to comfort them. And in return, I get to be loved by them.

5

Awareness

Now, more than ever, we must not let
cynicism, negativity,
or the busyness of life allow us to lose sight
of the good.

The Goodness Is Still Here

Catch a glimpse of joy—it comes to your bedside at 6:02 a.m. with disheveled hair and a wide-awake grin.
Catch a glimpse of promise—it rests peacefully on the sand, unbroken by the waves that tossed it ashore.
Catch a glimpse of unity—it is found at your neighbor's doorstep when you present a little something from your kitchen.

Catch a glimpse of devotion—it is seen in a threadbare stuffed animal clutched tightly in the hands of a child.
Catch a glimpse of loyalty—it resides in a wagging tail waiting patiently by the door when you arrive home.
Catch a glimpse of triumph—it is etched in the face of someone who runs a race she never thought she could.
Catch a glimpse of peace—it is gathered around a table after a crazy-busy day, your favorite voices talking all at once.
Catch a glimpse of safety—it is in your loved one's clothes in a pile on the floor below his sleeping face.
Now, more than ever, we must catch glimpses of that which can lift us up.
Now, more than ever, we must search for these barely noticeable glimmers of light that have the power to carry us.
Now, more than ever, we must not let cynicism, negativity, or the busyness of life allow us to lose sight of the good.
Because the goodness is still here.
Oh yes, the goodness is still here.
It arrives at your bedside at 6:02.
It curls up in your lap at the end of the day.
It reaches for your hand when you need something to hold on to.
Catch a glimpse and hold it. Hold it tightly. Let goodness prevail.

Today's Reminder

Today I will turn my attention away from the negativity filling my senses and my News Feed. I will turn to the people I love and notice that there is still so much goodness to be grasped and celebrated. Goodness comes down the stairs with crazy morning hair. It has a milk mustache and stinky feet. It puts gasoline in my car and kisses me good night. It bags my groceries with a smile. It teaches my children. It hugs me with shaky, wrinkled hands. The ability to detect goodness where others see nothing good is more than a day changer; it's a life changer. Today I will notice the good in the world and in my world.

6

Grace

Chances are you could take a little pressure off yourself, and things would still be okay.

CHANCES ARE

Chances are . . .
He'll remember your soothing whispers bringing comfort in the night, not your red-hot impatience that sometimes got the best of you.
Chances are . . .
She'll remember the way your soft arms gathered her up in the morning, not the puffiness of your eyes or the exhaustion in your voice.
Chances are . . .
She'll remember the new beginnings you offered when she messed up, not the stained couch cushions and perpetual dust bunnies.
Chances are . . .
He'll remember the way your eyes shined as he stood over his birthday cake, not whether the confection came from your kitchen or the store.
Chances are . . .
She'll remember the gift of your hand and your time as she walked along the curb, not the gifts the other kids got that she didn't.
Chances are . . .

He'll remember the sound of your laughter, not your embarrassing singing voice and horrible rhythm.
Chances are . . .
She'll remember the yesses you gave to feeding strays and jumping in puddles, not the noes to powdered sugar doughnuts and pet snakes.
Chances are he'll remember how you showed up.
Chances are she'll remember how you'd say, "I love you," out of the blue.
Chances are she'll remember how her pain was your pain.
Chances are you're better at this gig than you think you are.
Chances are you're pretty amazing in the eyes of those who love you.
Chances are you could take a little pressure off yourself, and things would still be okay.

Today's Reminder

Today I refuse to wallow in regret and guilt; I refuse to fall victim to comparison and self-judgment. Next week, next year, or ten years from now, my family will not remember what I made for dinner, whether it was from a box or homemade. They will not remember if the bathroom counter shone or if it was covered in globs of toothpaste. But they will remember if I laughed at the dinner table or hugged them fiercely at bedtime. Today I want them to remember my laugh and my hugs more than anything else. Thus, I will focus my energies on being a person fueled by joy, not a person burdened by regret.

7

Awareness

Just because a negative thought comes to
mind doesn't mean you have to speak it,

act on it,
or pass it on to someone you love.

LET IT GO

It's tempting to say, "I can't face another day,"
when there's so much heaviness to face.
But who said you have to face the day head-on?
Give it a loving glance; maybe you'll see a glimmer of goodness you didn't expect.

It's tempting to say, "I'm failing,"
when your life looks like a mess.
But who said you have to have it all together to believe progress is taking place?
Don't try to clean up the mess; look for the evidence of growth and goodness in the messy piles and broken pieces.

It's tempting to say, "Why do I even bother?"
when it feels as though nothing you do is reciprocated or appreciated.
But who said there's not an unspoken "Thank you" in the eyes of those who count on you?

It's tempting to say, "This is the last place I want to be,"
when you're stuck in a mind-numbing routine.
But who said you have to go on a tropical getaway to feel passion, energy, and enthusiasm?
Vacation moments can be found in a pair of cozy slippers, hot baths, or leaf-covered sidewalks if you put your heart and focus into it.

It's tempting to say, "I lost it again,"
when you think you're doing more damage than good.
But who said your meltdowns are being counted or tracked?
Before you throw yourself under the bus, acknowledge the hearty doses of love and presence you dole out every day.

It's tempting to think the worst, but that's not helpful or healing.
Your thoughts determine what's going to come out of your mouth, what's going to be your next move, and perhaps whether you're going to give up or hang on.
Your thoughts touch your loved ones and influence what they think, what comes out of their mouths, what steps they take, and perhaps even whether they give up or hang on.

Your thoughts are the first step toward a better day.

So the next time you're tempted to think the worst,
catch it,
hold it,
consider it.
Who says you have to listen?

Just because a critical thought comes to mind doesn't mean you have to speak it, act on it, or pass it on to someone you love.
Acknowledge your worst thought,
then let it go
so something hopeful and healing can take its place in your heart, mind, body, and home.

Today's Reminder

Today I refuse to give my inner critic so much power. Too often I let it take me down a negative path and prevent me from feeling hope, connection, and gratitude. My inner critic will be used as a cue to say something positive—to notice what I'm doing right or what's going right. When my inner critic pipes up and threatens to sabotage me, my people, my day, or my life, that's my cue—to come to my own defense and point out the goodness I know is in me and around me.

8

Gratitude

The ability to detect goodness where others
see no good
is more than a day changer; it's a life changer.

GRATITUDE UNDIVIDED

Have you ever been held in an embrace so warm you didn't want to let go?
Have you ever watched a sunset so beautiful you didn't want to see it disappear?
Have you ever heard a song so soothing you wished it could play forever?
Have you ever studied a face so intently you could see it with closed eyes?
That's gratitude of the purest form.
That's thankfulness void of distraction, judgment, or expectation.
That's appreciation you can feel deep down in your bones.

It can turn a floor littered with dirty clothes into a comforting reminder that your beloveds are home.
It can turn a grumpy face into a celebration of a child's lively spirit and spunk.
It can turn a string of bad luck into compassion for someone who is worse off.
It can turn a long wait into a chance to think without interruption.
It can turn a state of overwhelm into an opportunity to ask for help and lean on a friend.
It can turn a long, hard road into strength you didn't know you had.

This day might be filled with long waits, grouchy people, tough questions, and hopelessness; but there's an embrace, a sunset, a song, or a face that can bring temporary peace to your frenzied soul. Open your arms and your eyes and grasp a moment of *gratitude undistracted* and *thankfulness whole.*

Today's Reminder

There are moments when I am accepting of my life as it is, even though it is far from perfect. There are moments when I am accepting of who I am, even though I fall short on a regular basis. There are moments when I am accepting of my loved ones, despite their shortcomings and flaws. And those moments when I am most accepting of my life, myself, and my loved ones is when gratitude is in the forefront—not in the background, not an afterthought, not left behind in a hurried rush. Today I will put gratitude in the forefront so I can see what is good. Recognizing divine moments within this day is a surefire way to create more of them.

9

Grace

Right before my very eyes, I saw a
transformation take place in my child . . .
from wounded soul to hopeful survivor with
a chance at a beautiful future.

HEAL THE PAST, EXPAND THE FUTURE

I was combing out my child's wet hair when she began describing a memory from one night several years ago, a night when I was overwhelmed by the stress of my overly-distracted, maxed-out life.

As my then-five-year-old daughter reflected back on that night, the memory spilled from her lips as if it had been waiting for a chance to surface. She was clearly surprised by her emotional reaction, blinking back the tears and saying with embarrassment, "I can't believe this is making me cry."

I painfully watched her struggle to maintain her composure, and all I could think was this:

Never again will I wonder if the harsh tone of my voice is absorbed into her small ears and tender spirit.

Never again will I wonder if the "bad" memories are cataloged right along with the "good" in her memory bank.

Because now I know.

But this story is not about guilt, shame, or regret over things I cannot change. This story is about hope, because what happened next was pivotal.

I looked into my child's face and said the only words that could be said to a child who remembered the harsh words and actions of a maxed-out mother.

"I am sorry. I am so very sorry. Will you forgive me?"

Then, right before my very eyes, I saw a transformation take place in my child, who moved from wounded soul to hopeful survivor with a chance at a beautiful future. My child threw her whole body into her act of forgiveness by wrapping her arms tightly around my neck and whispering, "Oh yes, Mama. I forgive you."

Like there was ever any doubt.

Today's Reminder

For a moment, let me imagine my loved ones growing up never hearing the words, "I'm sorry." Let me imagine living with someone who never admits he messed up or she was wrong. Let me imagine how my loved ones would then view their own mistakes. The truth is this: being human allows my loved ones to be human. Getting back up after I fall down gives others courage to do the same. Asking for forgiveness lifts a weight—not only from my shoulders, but also from the shoulders of my beloveds. It gives us a chance to discuss what we wished we would have done differently and how we'll react in the future.

10

Awareness

I can't bear to let a spot go unkissed, a
word go unsaid,
or a strand of hair go untouched.

In a Lifetime

I'm guilty of making wagers with time.
I'll admit I don't always use time wisely.
I often squander it on superficial, meaningless things that
I deem "important."

Things that are not really important.
Lately, though, I've gotten some clarity.
It comes in the early morning hours when I must wake my child for the early arrival of her school bus.
It is still dark outside, so I creep into her room.
Waking a sleeping child goes against every fiber of my being.
I pause for a moment
and watch her at peace.
As I study her face peeking out from under the covers, I barter with time. But it's different than before. Because in that moment, I can see clearly what I need more time to do.
There's a spot on her face I have yet to kiss.
There's a freckle on her nose I have yet to count.
There's a place on her back I have yet to scratch.
There's a laugh in her chest I have yet to hear.
There's a smile on her face I have yet to see.
There's a dream in her heart I have yet to encourage.
There's a word of love I have yet to say.
There's an apology I have yet to give.
There's an embrace I have yet to offer.
So I need more time.
Because I can't bear to let a spot to go unkissed, a word go unsaid, or a strand of hair go untouched.
Not in this lifetime.
Not in her lifetime.
Today I will be thankful for the time that I am given.
I will spend it on what is most important
in a lifetime.

Today's Reminder

Some days I find it hard to slow down and be fully present with my beloved people. They want me to stay a little longer, and it is all I can do to oblige. Sometimes when I say no to a little extra time, I wish I could say yes. If that happens today, I will say yes. In my head, I will agree to fifty more seconds. I will count to fifty in my head, if necessary. By mustering a little extra time, it might give my beloved a chance to say something important or funny, or to simply whisper, "I love you." If that happens, I will be thankful I stayed. I will be thankful I did not miss it by rushing off. With just an extra fifty seconds, I can savor time and walk away fulfilled.

11

Grace

Love, forgiveness, and grace will be the fiber that holds this day, this family, this one precious life together when it threatens to come apart at the seams.

CLOSER THAN I WAS BEFORE

My angry words spilled out. I spoke too soon. Morning stressors got the best of me.
But I didn't let guilt consume me the way I used to.
I said I was sorry and asked to begin again.
That's progress.
I am closer than I was before.

My inner perfectionist reared its ugly head. I compared. I criticized. I told myself it wasn't good enough.
But then my heart spoke up and said, "Stop. You're doing the best you can right now."
I looked past the mess and the mayhem and saw the flowers instead of the weeds.
That's progress.
I am closer than I was before.

My day was too packed. I overscheduled. I underloved. I was too rushed, too hurried, too frenzied.
But then I stopped in the middle of the chaos and removed the ticking clock weighing heavily on my soul.
I touched the fading summer freckles on my daughter's nose and felt the pressure wane.
That's progress.
I am closer than I was before.

Every second is not about grasping what matters, but now I have awareness I didn't have before.
I am only human.
I am learning.
Love, forgiveness, and grace will be the fiber that holds this day, this family, this one precious life together when it threatens to come apart at the seams.
That's progress.
I am closer than I was before.

Today's Reminder

Today I release myself from judgment. I will not view the mistakes of yesterday as failures but instead as stepping-stones to the lovingly imperfect, grace-filled life I've always wanted to live. Who I am becoming matters more than who I once was. Today matters more than yesterday.

12

Awareness

Life's parade is happening right now. Candy might not be falling from the sky, but keep looking. Keep looking. Something good is just around the bend.

LIFE'S PARADE

They parade before me with toothless smiles and contagious laughter.
They parade into my room at midnight with tummy aches and tears.
They parade before me all happy and shiny in their back-to-school clothes. *Is it really this time?* I say to myself.

They parade into the bathroom. "Whatcha doing?" they ask.
They parade before me with beautiful artwork made just for me.
They parade into my space with morning breath and excessive grumpiness.
They parade before me with caps and gowns. *Is it really this time?* I say to myself.

They parade before me with wilted bouquets, mosquito bites, and dirty knees.
They parade before me with hope shining in their sparkly eyes.
They parade before me with excitement about little things I would fail to see without their hands pulling me to a stop.

I'm slowly learning life can be a parade.
Not always a sunny-day parade.
Not always the kind that tosses out sweet candy, colorful beads, and friendly waves.
Not always the kind with beautifully adorned floats and unpoppable balloons.

Life's parade is not like that. It definitely has its highlights, but they don't come around every bend. Oh no. Life's parade can be redundant. It can be tedious, frustrating, and downright painful at times. You can look ahead and feel like there's nothing beautiful in sight.

Keep looking. Keep looking.

Just when you're about to throw in the towel, a glimmer of goodness will come along. "Oh my, that's beautiful," you will say. "That was worth the wait," you will say. And then you will look forward to the next highlight, hoping it will come soon.

Keep looking. Keep looking.

Life's parade is happening right now. Candy might not be falling from the sky, but don't let that discourage you. Something good is just around the bend.

Today's Reminder

Today will be filled with many invitations. I cannot say yes to all of them, so I will say yes to certain ones; I will say yes to the invitations that make someone I love happy. It might sound like this: Yes, you can throw a penny in the fountain. Yes, we can read one more book. Yes, we should have a date night! Yes, we can go grab a coffee. *I will then notice the joy that yes brings to my loved ones; that joy is mine for the taking; that joy is the candy in the parade of life. I will lift my hands to the sky and be thankful I didn't miss joy's invitation.*

13

Grace

Even when it's hard to stand, there's still so
much goodness to see.
I hope you rise.
I hope you rise.

I AM HERE

I'd been in bed all day in severe pain from surgery. The sun beckoned me relentlessly to bask in it before it was gone. So when the pain finally relented, I suggested my children get out the Slip 'N Slide. I offered to watch. Guilt told me I should help them hammer in the stakes or at least help with the hose. Guilt wanted to remind me I'd missed the whole day. Guilt said I should have at least combed my hair or brushed my teeth before coming outside.

It was really all I could do to put on some clothes.

It was really all I could do to get myself out the door.

So this is what I said to Guilt—in case someone out there is in need of a comeback—because the inner critic can be persistent, mean-spirited, and wrong. Totally wrong.

I said,

I am here.
I am here.
Not shiny,
not whole—a little broken, actually.
But I am here. I am here managing a smile.
I'm not conversational, but I'm observant. My eyes are on them and they see me watching.
I am here.

"Watch this, Mama," they kept saying, knowing they had all of me.

And so I watched. I watched my growing babies with their strong legs and open-mouthed laughter, and I laughed a little too.

I could not play.

I could not join in.

But I was there. I was there.

And with each trip down the Slip 'N Slide, truth and perspective quieted Guilt's misleading voice in my head, directing me back to what was most important.

I am here.

I am here.

And that is enough. That is more than enough.

Today, no matter what battle we face, let's not allow Guilt to skew the truth or obstruct our view.

Even when it's hard to stand, there's still so much goodness to see.

I hope you rise.

I hope you rise.

Today's Reminder

My loved ones are not counting my mistakes. They're not documenting the date and time of every failure. They're not noting my flaws and imperfections. They're more focused on my helpful hands, my faithfulness, my familiar scent, my love, and my presence. Today is not about what I didn't do or who I'm not; it's about the fact I am here, in the flesh, arms wide open, ready to love.

14

Gratitude

Today let me appreciate the gifts in the mundane, ordinary moments that are graciously given to me. Because even though it's far from perfect, even though sometimes it's messy and hard, this is my one precious life.

APPRECIATING MY LIFE

I fail to appreciate the feeling of her small body in footy pajamas until she suddenly outgrows them and declares, "I want regular pajamas—ones that don't have feet."

Today let me appreciate the perfect size and shape she is right now.

Let me appreciate my child.

I fail to appreciate those odd mannerisms that drive me crazy until we are separated for a time, and suddenly I long to hear one of those silly quirks.

Today let me appreciate the gum chewing, the knuckle cracking, and even the humming, because when I hear these things I know I am in the company of my love.

Let me appreciate my spouse.

I fail to appreciate the richness of my life until I walk down the busy street and see sadness on the fringes—those with empty hands, empty eyes, and empty souls.

Today let me appreciate the fact that I have known love in my life, and let me share it with those who have not.

Let me appreciate the value of spreading kindness.

I fail to appreciate the wrinkles, the bulges, and the sags until I reflect on all I have endured to be where I am today.

Today let me appreciate each beautiful experience of my life that is etched across my face and body.

Let me appreciate that I am alive.

I fail to appreciate the value of a familiar face until I find myself in a new city, a new town, and everyone I meet is a stranger.

Today let me appreciate long-time friendships that time and distance cannot alter.

Let me appreciate a familiar face.

I fail to appreciate the value of a safe drive home until I see blinding headlights and hear the scrape of metal against metal.

Today let me appreciate my safe drive home and those precious faces peering back at me in my rearview mirror.

Let me appreciate my security.

Today let me appreciate the sun—even when it's behind the clouds.

Today let me appreciate the good-byes—even if they're not our last.

Today let me appreciate the goodness—even if I have to dig a little to find it.

Today let me appreciate the gifts in the mundane, ordinary moments that are graciously given to me. Because even though it's far from perfect, even though sometimes it's messy and hard, this is my one precious life.

For this anything-but-small miracle that is my life, I am thankful.

Today's Reminder

Rather than complaining about my unpleasant experiences and feelings today, I will thank them. This is called being a Silver Lining Spotter. *From that place of gratitude, I am more likely to find a momentary* glimmer of goodness, *reminding me that the whiny, messy, unpredictable moments of life are not all bad. In fact, they are what make home a home and a life a life. Doing this gratitude practice out loud will show my loved ones how to be* Silver Lining Spotters *too. Not only will this practice improve the temperature of my heart and home; it will also provide my loved ones with beneficial coping skills for life.*

15

GRACE

Someday, maybe sooner than we think, every sacrifice we ever made and every tear we ever cried will be exchanged for something wondrous.

FREE FROM THE HEAVY

There are days when we want to beat our heads against the wall, when we scream into our pillows, and leave tears upon the steering wheel.

There are days when we feel there is no more left to give, when we want to throw in the towel and admit, "I can't do this anymore."

There are days when the words spoken in our heads are words we never want another soul to hear.

There are days when we feel like we've made too many mistakes to ever be redeemed.

Those days are not pretty.

But despite the failures, the missteps, the doubts, the inner turmoil we experience, we do something extraordinary.

We show up.

And we keep showing up.

Because we know someone is counting on us.

When that someone sees us showing up, it means more than we even know.

Someday, maybe sooner than we think, every sacrifice we ever made and every tear we ever cried will be exchanged for something wondrous. It might be a tender word, an apologetic embrace, an expression of joy—whatever it is, we will know because it is the moment we've been waiting for, perhaps praying for.

In that moment, we will shine for the one we love, and the one we love will shine for us.

Every past mistake that once weighed heavily on our souls will be overshadowed by the light of a beautiful moment in time.

At last, we will be free from the heavy.

Today's Reminder

Today I will focus on where I build up, not where I fall short. Today I will focus on where I shine, not where I stumble. Today I will focus on what I contribute, not what I take away. Each time I see the worst rather than the best in myself, something of great value is diminished. I am worthy of kind, gentle, and loving consideration. Today I will see myself through the eyes of love.

16

Gratitude

If at first you don't see the value, you might be looking at things from the wrong angle.

WHAT YOU CAN'T PUT A PRICE ON

It was my daughter's final month of preschool. I opened her school folder to find an 8 x 10 class picture and an order form. The instructions read, "If you would like to keep the school picture, send thirteen dollars in the envelope provided. Otherwise, please return the picture."

I stared at the photo for a moment, trying to consider why I would pay thirteen dollars for the photo.

I saw a fake smile on my child.

I saw squints from the glaring sun.

I saw a group of children who looked as if they wished they were somewhere else.

I saw a waste of money.

I did not even hesitate as I put the picture back into my daughter's folder to return to school. The next morning she came to me with the picture in hand. "Why did you put this back, Mama?" she asked in a distraught, shaky voice.

I told her that thirteen dollars seemed like a lot of money for a picture. Then I pointed to the squinting faces and added, "Plus, the smiles aren't that good."

Now there were tears sliding down her cheeks. "How can you give it back?" she cried. "It has my teacher in it."

No explanation, no justification, no convincing words—just one powerful, undeniable sentiment: *this picture has my beloved teacher in it.*

There are some things you just can't put a price on.

A few days later, my family found ourselves huddled against the concrete wall of our basement, awaiting news of the projected path of the mile-wide tornado that had caused massive devastation in the city west of us. The radio announcer said the name of the small town where my daughter's teacher lived. I hoped my daughter's determination to keep the class photo was not some sort of premonition of what was about to come.

I sent a text message to her teacher, telling her how much we loved her and that we prayed for her safety. I couldn't breathe as I waited for her response.

At last, it came. She was in a tornado shelter. She was safe.

There are some things you just can't put a price on.

That class picture is now five years old, but it still sits on my daughter's dresser. When I look at it, I see the face of a woman who loved, nurtured, educated, and protected my most precious gift for a year of her life. I didn't see the value in the picture before because I had been looking at it from the wrong angle. But through the eyes of my child, I learned there are just some things you can't put a price on.

Today's Reminder

Today I will resist the urge to let society define what is successful, valuable, beautiful, or worthy by appearance, achievements, awards, celebrity endorsements, or price. I will consider attributes such as courage, effort, honesty, patience, determination, risk-taking, and compassion when evaluating someone or something's value. Today I will use meaningful measures, open eyes, and an open heart to determine worth.

17

Gratitude

Finding the good in bad situations becomes a passageway—a passageway toward celebrating, rather than grumbling away your precious life.

A PASSAGEWAY

Something happens when the world's longest red light
becomes a chance to breathe and think a grateful thought.
Something happens when that exhausting bedtime plea

becomes a chance to say the loving words you forgot to say in the rush of the day.
Something happens when that painful rejection becomes a chance to reassess and go after something even better.
Something happens when that perpetual dark cloud becomes a chance to appreciate the sunlight in a way you never did before.
Something happens when that careless mistake becomes a chance to offer the grace you always wondered if you could give.
Something happens when that tragedy a little too close to home becomes a chance to acknowledge the blessing of health and security.
Something happens when you begin to see life's inconveniences, challenges, and hardships
not as inconveniences, challenges, and hardships
but as
perspective givers,
golden opportunities,
second chances.
Finding the good in bad situations becomes a passageway—a passageway to becoming
a little more grateful,
a little more patient,
a little more loving,
than you were yesterday.
Finding the good in bad situations becomes a passageway—a passageway toward celebrating, rather than grumbling away your precious life.

Today's Reminder

Today I challenge myself to find one positive in the daily disappointments, frustrations, and failures. Once I find that silver lining, I predict it will be easier to move on or come up with Plan B. Finding a silver lining in a dismal situation becomes a passageway leading me from frustration and skepticism toward a place of hope and gratitude. From the edge of the silver lining is where I will see today's blessings most clearly.

18

Grace

I am ready to live my life doing what I know is right for me. I am ready to immerse myself in what makes me happy, fulfilled, and alive. I am ready to make mistakes and get back up. I am ready to be unapologetically me.

SURRENDER TO BE FREE

There is freedom in throwing on your favorite hat when the children's laughter calls.
There is freedom in saying "This is good enough for today" and letting perfection go.
There is freedom in being real, flawed, and courageous.
There is freedom in not doing what "everyone else" does.
There is freedom in lingering hugs and open-mouthed laughter.
There is freedom in all-day pajamas and no schedule.
There is freedom in being unavailable to the world so you can be available to those who mean the most.
There is freedom in
cloud gazing,
apple picking,
leaf jumping,
and sunset watching.

There is freedom in campfires and storytelling under the stars.
There is freedom in noticing everyday miracles when you used to rush on by.
In order to find this most liberating type of freedom, you must be ready—ready to surrender the hope of being liked and accepted by everyone. You must surrender the fear of making mistakes. You must surrender the tendency to make decisions based on what other people think.
I don't know about you, but I am ready to surrender. I am ready to immerse myself in what makes me happy, fulfilled, and alive. I am ready to make mistakes and get back up. I am ready to be unapologetically me.
And now that I've surrendered, something miraculous has happened.
A weight has been lifted.
My shoulders and head are being held higher.
My voice embodies a new confidence.
So even if it's just for one day,
stop running,
stop pushing,
stop achieving,
stop perfecting,
stop critiquing,
stop belittling,
stop blaming.
Instead, *surrender* and be free with the ones who make life worth living.

Today's Reminder

I want to be a joyful and present participant in the party that is my life. In those moments when I peel off the manager name tag—forgo the rules, reject the grown-up ways and choose to be silly—connection happens. In my loved ones' eyes, I become a real person who is easier to talk to and more enjoyable to be around. Today—if only for a few minutes—I will resist the urge to be in charge, organize, plan, clean, or dictate. I will forgo the mirror, throw on a hat, and slip on comfy shoes made for adventuring. I will say yes to someone else cracking the eggs or wearing pajamas to the store. I will use a silly voice. I will turn up the music and dance in the car. The words "Not today" will be replaced with "Why not today?" I will be the party *and watch someone's face light up at the sight of me letting go in order to grasp a little joy. (It might even be my own.)*

19

AWARENESS

Every human being, young or old, has a heart's bulletin board. Every person needs safety, love, and affirmation offered in terms he or she can understand.

THE HEART'S BULLETIN BOARD

When I consider the challenges my loved one will face, and the unknown territories she will have to navigate, my prayer is that I will be around to guide, encourage, and support her as each troubling situation arises. Alas, the days are full. There is only so much time to talk, teach, respond, and listen. The number of days I have to be a guiding force in my dear one's life are beyond my control, but today is not beyond my control. Today I have time, even if it is just a few moments, to pin messages on her heart that I hope will stick indefinitely.

Today, a pin for love:

You make my day better.

I love spending time with you.

You amaze me. You honestly do.

Today, a pin for safety:

Trust your instincts.

You can use me as an excuse to say no to something that is unsafe.

Be alert when you walk anywhere in public—don't look down at your phone.

Today, a pin for affirmation:

I admire the way you handled that disappointing situation.

I enjoy hearing what you think about this. Tell me more.

You came up with a smart plan to get that project accomplished.

Unlike an actual corkboard that hangs upon a wall, the heart's bulletin board can never become too full. There is endless room, especially for soul-building words and life-giving messages. There is no age requirement. Every human being, young or old, has a heart's bulletin board. Every person needs safety, love, and affirmation offered in terms he or she can understand.

We have no control over how many pins we will be allowed to give in our lifetime, so let us pin as many as we can today.

Pin grace.

Pin adoration.

Pin wisdom.

Pin appreciation.

Pin wisdom.

Pin encouragement.

Pin forgiveness.

Pin love. Pin lots and lots of love, every chance you get.

Today's Reminder

I cannot control the troubling situations my loved ones will encounter throughout their lives, but hope is not lost. By offering words of wisdom and encouragement as part of our daily routine, I can prepare their hearts for what they might someday face. Even if I am not physically standing beside them, my loved ones can still hear these life-giving, life-saving messages in times of fear, frustration, worry, despair, or hopelessness if I say them often enough.

20

AWARENESS

In the midst of our busy, media-saturated,
overscheduled lives,
taking time to really know someone is the
ultimate act of love.

KNOWING YOU IS LOVING YOU

The morning after my older daughter turned double digits, I caught a glimpse of her that left me gripping the kitchen counter and struggling to breathe. It was all I could do not to grab her and never let her go. In that moment, something became crystal clear. I knew exactly what I wanted to do with the remaining time I am given, before I am staring at a mature young woman who seems only vaguely familiar. I wanted to say to her . . .

I want to read your words before they are kept under lock and key for your eyes only.

I want to watch you laugh until tears come to your eyes before I am no longer your favorite audience.

I want to admire your choice of color combination and accessories before my opinion on fashion is politely ignored.

I want to listen to your nighttime secrets before the

bedroom door shuts, and I'm standing outside listening to your favorite song drift out from beneath the crack.

I want to look into your eyes and ask, "What's on your mind?" before I am no longer privy to your hopes, dreams, worries, and fears.

I want to say yes before your invitations are reserved for people your own age.

I just want to know you, really know you, as you grow.

With each passing year, the map of my child's life expands to reveal a new section of uncharted territory. And although it might be tempting to retreat to separate paths, separate rooms, and separate screens, I must stay the course. This means I must accept the rare and important invitations that may sound like this:

"Hey, Mom, check this out."

"I want to show you something, Mom."

"Wanna see what I've been doing?"

I must hear things that are not going to be easy to hear.

I must answer questions that are not easy to answer.

I must love a child who may not always be easy to love.

If I make a conscious effort to accept her invitations now, perhaps I will still receive them as she grows; I can only try.

Whether we are in familiar or unfamiliar territory, one thing remains constant: she is my child, and I will love her as much as humanly possible in the time I am given.

On the days I feel I'm staring at a stranger, I will try more than ever to be all there—because in the midst of our busy, media-saturated, overscheduled lives, taking time to really know someone is the ultimate act of love.

Today's Reminder

In those moments when I feel distraction tightening its grip on my life, I will envision the future relationship I want to have with my child.

Although time with her is not a tangible item I can check off a list, spending time with her now is a priceless investment in the future. With such efforts to push away distraction and offer my attention, my child's recollection of her childhood might someday be this:

My mom looked at me when we talked. She was never too busy to listen to what I had to say. My mom's eye contact made me feel important and worthy. I liked sharing my thoughts and ideas with her. I turned to her when I had a problem or when I had good news to share. I wanted to tell my mom things because I could always count on her to listen—listen with her eyes, heart, and soul. And now, even though I am grown, she is still the person I want to talk to when I have something to share.

21

Awareness

We are all just waiting for someone to notice—notice our pain, notice our scars, notice our fear, notice our joy, notice our triumphs, notice our courage, and the one who notices is a rare and beautiful gift.

The Noticer

My daughter handed me her school progress report. Although it displayed a stream of positive check marks, one check mark stood dejectedly alone from the rest.

"How am I doing, Mom?" Avery asked with a level of maturity that did not match the small, disheveled person gazing up at me with pink spectacles teetering on the tip of her nose. With her finger, she pointed to her teacher's neatly printed words next to the lone check mark.

It read: *Distracted in large groups*. I already knew this. I knew this long before it was written on an official report card. Since she was a toddler, this child has offered astute observations of the world around her.

After pointing out all the positives on the progress report, I told her what was written next to that one check mark.

Upon hearing the news, she gave me a tiny, uncertain smile and shyly admitted, "I do look around a lot."

But before my child could feel one ounce of shame, one iota of failure, I came down on bended knee and looked her straight in the eyes. I didn't want her to just *hear* these words, I wanted her to *feel* them. This is what I said:

> *Yes. You do look around a lot. You noticed Sam sitting off by himself with a skinned knee on the field trip, and you comforted him.*
>
> *You noticed Banjo the cat had a runny nose, and the veterinarian said it was a good thing we brought him in when we did.*
>
> *You noticed our waitress was working really hard and suggested we leave an extra good tip.*
>
> *You noticed Grandpa was walking slower than the rest of us, so you waited for him.*
>
> *You notice the beautiful view every time we cross the bridge to go to swim practice.*
>
> *And you know what? I don't ever want you to stop noticing, because you are a Noticer. And the Noticers of the world are rare and beautiful gifts.*

As I watched my daughter beam with the glow of acceptance, I realized her approach to life had the power to change the world.

You see, we are all just waiting for someone to notice—notice our pain, notice our scars, notice our fear, notice our joy, notice our triumphs, notice our courage.

And the one who notices is a rare and beautiful gift.

Let us all be Noticers today.

Someone is just waiting for us to notice the goodness inside.

Today's Reminder

Today I will try my best to love others the way I want to be loved—with understanding, kindness, empathy, and grace. I will try to love them with the kind of love that comes from walking in their shoes. Perhaps this approach will lessen feelings of isolation, failure, inadequacy, and shame. Perhaps this will result in fewer acts of violence and more acts of kindness. By loving others right where they are, just as they are, I can create a ripple of kindness and make a positive difference in the world.

22

Awareness

If I wait on the world to tell me when to stop, I never will.

If I Wait on the World

I'll never forget listening to a talented trio called The Millionaire's Club on a busy street corner in Seattle's Pike Place Market. My ukulele-playing daughter was mesmerized by the musicians. After watching intently for a few minutes, I could tell she was not going to be ready to move on anytime soon. I squatted down, and she took that as an invitation to sit on my lap. After listening for a few more minutes, her tapping foot suddenly stopped. She turned and whispered into my ear, "I don't want to forget this."

Because words failed me, I just hugged her tighter. I knew with certainty that neither of us would forget this unexpected moment in time. As people rushed past, going where they needed to go, I had an epiphany.

If I wait on the world to tell me when to stop, I never will.

If I wait for the perfect moment to take a break, I never will.

If I wait to live life until the duties are done, I never will.

But if I can take pause on one of the busiest street corners in the country and connect to the one I love, I must make a point to do it at home.

And this is what I've found: *There are moments in between the duties and busyness of life that can be made sacred.* Meals at the kitchen table, carpooling to practice, morning send-offs, and nightly tuck-ins all hold great potential—potential to be *all there.* Within the responsibilities of life, there are opportunities to meet her gaze, to ask her questions, to listen to her thoughts, to sit beside her as she does something she enjoys.

I used to believe our fondest memories were made in the grand occasions of life. But now I know they happen when we take pause in the ordinary, mundane moments of a busy day. Now I know the most meaningful life experiences don't happen in the "when," they happen in the "now."

No longer will I wait for the world to slow down before I give myself permission to be right where I am.

It is the sacred pauses of life that bring gratitude to my heart and heal my frenzied soul.

Today's Reminder

At least one time today, I will ignore the ticking clock weighing down my soul—the one always rushing me forward. With the whisper, "Don't forget this," I will give myself permission to be right where I am. Each time I triumph over my rushing ways, my frenzied soul will exhale. Today I will not let life's subtle moments get lost in the shuffle where they have no chance of being appreciated or becoming memories.

23

Gratitude

When I look for "flowers" instead of
"weeds" in my daily life,
blessings become more obvious,
and perspective comes within reach.

SEE FLOWERS, NOT WEEDS

Yes, the weekend was too busy (weeds) and I didn't get as much rest as I'd like, but all the activities gave us time together as a family (flowers).

I wouldn't want anyone else to be there for the games, practices, performances, or family errands but me.

Yes, I feel like I just did these dishes, made these lunches, and washed these clothes (weeds), but I am feeding and clothing those who are most precious to me (flowers).

I wouldn't want anyone else caring for my family.

Yes, there is a mess in every room of the house (weeds), but it is evidence that my family spent time playing, laughing, creating, and living (flowers).

I wouldn't want a pristine house with no signs of life.

Yes, she wore shoes caked with mud to school (weeds), but the joy on her face as she scoured the pumpkin patch and found the perfect pumpkin was unforgettable (flowers).

I wouldn't change a thing about my messy, joyful child.

When I look for flowers instead of weeds in my daily life, blessings become more obvious, and perspective comes within reach. Although it is often imperfect, exhausting, messy, and monotonous, I wouldn't trade my life or my people for anything.

Today's Reminder

Being the mistake monitor makes it hard to breathe. Predicting every problem and planning every outcome makes it hard to breathe. Overreacting to honest mishaps and inconveniences makes it hard to breathe. Today I will strive to be less of a dictator and more of a guiding, supportive, loving presence. By noticing the flowers instead of the weeds, I will go to bed feeling lighter and happier. This may lead to a better morning—one where I feel grateful to love and care for the people in my life.

24

Grace

Let us gather as much happiness as we can to sustain us in the days and years ahead.

GATHERING HAPPINESS

Becoming distracted from what truly matters in life is easy in this high-resolution, overly pressured, picture-perfect world we live in. With each new season, the onslaught of trendy new fashions, stylish home décor, succulent recipes, and cutesy crafts sometimes cause me to question my Hands Free Life. My messy, imperfect existence is a stark contrast to the images featured in glossy magazines and in my News Feed.

Grasping what really matters means living life by heart, not by the expectations society airbrushes for me. It is my greatest hope that placing value on what really matters now will reflect in my children's future lives—in the way they connect, love, and create their own family traditions.

As my daughters joyfully lugged their misshapen pumpkins across a muddy field one afternoon, I caught a glimpse of the future that motivates me daily to keep filling the spaces of our lives with authentic connection.

I envisioned my grown daughters calling their children to the back porch to carve a massive pumpkin. As everyone pondered what expression the orange gourd should have, Natalie said, "I think the pumpkin should be happy. Mom always said fall was about gathering as much happiness as you can." I prayed she would someday continue with something like this:

> *My mom let me cook a lot—mostly so she wouldn't have to. She always wore her hair in a ponytail and went days without showering, but somehow she managed to smell good when she cuddled up next to me at bedtime. Mom didn't have time to decorate the house or make cutesy foods, but she always had time to listen. She wasn't into Monopoly or puzzles, but she'd get really excited about taking bike rides and going for walks. She'd always beg me to do my British accent, and then she would laugh until she had to run to the bathroom. Mom wasn't the most punctual at signing and returning school papers, but she never missed divine signs in nature. She was always the first to spot rainbows or sky crosses. I remember one fall night when she told me she was sorry she spent too much time worrying about things being perfect when I was little. Then she told me that my sister and I were the ones who taught her that being happy on the inside matters more than having things look perfect on the outside.*

As for today, our flowerpots may not be filled with bright orange mums, but we're filling our days with love and forgiveness. In doing so, we're gathering as much happiness as we can to sustain us in the days and years ahead.

Today's Reminder

Today I refuse to let outside pressures guilt me into saying yes to buying, entertaining, decorating, and scheduling things I want to decline. Saying yes only turns my time, energy, and focus away from what matters most. Today I will decline one request that will make me happier. It might sound like one of these three refusals: (1) No, that doesn't work for me right now; (2) I wish I could, but I can't; (3) It's no for today, but please ask me another time. *After I say no, I will note the feeling of relief that freeing word brings. I will commend myself for guarding my time and energy for what matters most to me.*

25

Awareness

My love for her is fixed. And it fixes me.

THE CERTAINTY OF LOVE

My daughter's school bus comes early, and I have the privilege of going into her room to wake her up. I call this duty a privilege because in the morning light, I can see a glimmer of the baby she once was.

As I leaned down to kiss her gently on the forehead the other morning, I thought to myself, *I'll never get tired of kissing this face. Never.*

This feeling of absolute certainty gave me an unexpected sense of calm.

Yes, she may be growing up, but my love for her will never change. I am certain of that.

As the day went on, I noticed other actions—performed in the name of love—that would never change, no matter how grown she is, no matter how much we disagree, no matter what unfortunate circumstances might come our way.

I'll never stop watching as she walks away from me.
I'll never stop imagining what is to become of her.
I'll never tire of that open-mouthed laugh that sounds like pure joy.
I'll never tire of watching her care for animals or sing "Amazing Grace."
I'll never stop noticing new freckles that pop up on her nose.
I'll never stop worrying when she is on a field trip or traveling without me.
I'll never stop wanting to know what's going on in that observant mind of hers.
I'll never stop wanting to protect her from disappointment, heartbreak, embarrassment, or harm.
I'll never stop kissing her forehead.

In an ever-changing world with little permanence, I am finding great comfort in the certainty of my love for this child.

I mourned the day she stopped playing with her beloved Polly Pocket dolls. She doesn't like dressy dresses anymore. The girl who once thought toothpaste was too spicy now tries sushi and hot barbecue sauce. The child who was afraid to dive off the blocks jumps in with a little too much fearlessness now. She is not scared of thunderstorms anymore and goes downstairs in the middle of the night to get a drink when she is thirsty.

In a face that seems to elongate with each passing day,
in a mind that expands every day with new ideas, hopes, and dreams,

in a body that grows stronger and longer each time she
crawls out of bed,
I am finding great comfort.
I am finding comfort in the stability of my love for this
child.
I can't predict much, but I can predict my love for her will
endure harsh elements, discord, distance, and time. This
I know for sure.
Perhaps it is one of the few things on earth that is eternal.
My love for her is fixed. And it fixes me.

Today's Reminder

I spend too much time wondering if I am enough: if I love enough, care enough, achieve enough. That ends today. I have proof of my significance: it is written on my loved ones' faces when they spot me sitting in the stands, clapping in the audience, or waiting curbside. My love is their reference point—a place in their hearts and minds where they feel loved and safe when faced with moments of uncertainty, nervousness, and fear. Today I will stop worrying about doing all the things *right in this lifetime. Instead, I'll focus on doing* one thing *right: a little love today. Because it's the love that sustains them. Love prevails over failures, flaws, and imperfect days.*

26

Gratitude

*Even on the hardest days, even in the most
challenging moments,
I can see tiny glimmers of goodness if I look
closely for them.*

THANK YOU, NOT-SO-PLEASANT MOMENT

Thank you, hurried morning. It is in the hunt for shoes, library books, and backpacks that I appreciate the slow Saturday. I will pay attention and appreciate the slow Saturday.

Thank you, perpetually dirty house. It is in finding rumpled sheets, toothpaste blobs, and abandoned socks that I appreciate the evidence of life being lived. I will pay attention.

Thank you, growing older. It is in finding another gray hair and another laugh line that I appreciate the blessings of another day. I will pay attention and appreciate another day.

Thank you, free-spirited child. It is in experiencing everything a little faster, a little louder, and a little riskier that I appreciate the courage it takes to be bold. I will pay attention and appreciate being bold.

Thank you, sensitive child. It is in experiencing everything a little deeper and a little more quietly that I see the gift of a tender heart. I will pay attention and appreciate the tender heart.

Thank you, pang of guilt. It is in wishing I did things differently that I appreciate the opportunity of second chances. I will pay attention and appreciate second chances.

Thank you, disappointment. It is in experiencing letdowns that I appreciate the fact that I had the courage to try. I will pay attention and appreciate the courage to try.

Thank you, daily challenges. It is in looking straight into the face of sorrow, struggle, fear, frustration, heartache, and worry that I appreciate the fact that I keep showing up. I will pay attention and appreciate the fact that I keep showing up.

And I will keep showing up.

Because even on the hardest days, even in the most challenging moments, I can see tiny glimmers of goodness if I look closely for them.

So today, I will pay attention and appreciate any glimmers of goodness I can find.

Today's Reminder

Today I release myself from trying to have everything figured out. Things are not where I want them to be, but that doesn't mean they won't get there. I will surrender the need to create a certain outcome and place my trust in God that things will work out as they should in time. Perhaps it will be even better than I expected or imagined.

27

Gratitude

I want to close my eyes in gratitude.
I want to open them in wonder.

VOW TO BREATHE

I don't want to feel like I am running late.
I don't want to feel like I will never catch up.
I don't want to multitask this day away.

I don't want to brush past the people I love.
I don't want to feel depleted and overwhelmed.
I don't want to fill every space of my day with "stuff."

Today I want to say yes to listening and laughter.
I want to remember what my heart loves to do and do it—
even for just a little bit.
I want to close my eyes in gratitude.
I want to open them in wonder.

I want to read a book.
I want to plant a seed.
I want to say, "Take your time," and mean it.

I want to give a good kiss.
I want to leave a surprise note.
I want to do a little bit of absolutely nothing.

I want to
rest,
dance,
laugh,
play.

I want to fill the spaces of my life with love.
So I can breathe
and maybe laugh a time or two.

Today's Reminder

Pausing to engrave life's most meaningful moments into our memory banks—this is living. Pausing to acknowledge the urgings of our hearts—this is living. Pausing when the whole world keeps on going—this is living. Let me pause to breathe life into today.

28

Awareness

In the end, a moment of exasperation will
be as much of a gift as a moment of joy,
only without the pretty packaging.

EVERY NOW AND THEN

Every now and then, I experience Hands Free reminders—moments when my child suddenly looks grown up or says something profound, moments when time slaps me in the face and says, "Pay attention. This won't last forever."

Every now and then, I need to be reminded that having to sweep up the crumbs beneath her chair is not really a "problem."

I need to be reminded that the times when she grasps my hand as we cross a busy street or says, "C'mere and see this ladybug" are moments to stop and savor.

I need to be reminded that I could complain less, cherish more, let go of the to-do's and say yes more often.

Because the day will come sooner than I think, the day when I will stand inside her bedroom closet and be able to see the floor. There will be no brightly colored garments haphazardly hung along the narrow walls, no dirty clothes that missed the mark of the laundry hamper.

I will place my hand on all that is left. And when I do, I will be so grateful that I hugged her that day rather than scolding her for writing her name on the wall of the closet.

In the end, a moment of exasperation will be as much of a gift as a moment of joy, only without the pretty packaging.

Today's Reminder

Today I will not look back in regret. Whether it was a mistake from yesterday or ten years ago, it is in the past. Dwelling on it or berating myself for it comes with a cost. It sabotages the opportunity of this *moment—to make a memory, to create a loving connection, or to feel joy in my soul. Often, I am the only one standing in the way of a new beginning. Today I will not stand in my own way. Today is a new beginning. I will grasp it with both hands.*

29

Awareness

Let this question guide your actions and
improve your day:
What do they really need?

WHAT THEY REALLY NEED

He needs that permission slip signed.
She needs bigger shoes—she's growing like a weed.
He needs to be at practice fifteen minutes early.
She needs to bring cookies to the party.
He needs to return the book by Tuesday.

But what do they *really* need?

Sometimes within the flurry and frenzy of the day,
I forget what they really need. I forget what *I* really need.

He needs quiet time to hear his thoughts and plot his dreams.
She needs to know I love her, no matter what she does or
doesn't do.
He needs my time.
She needs me to listen to every word.
He needs a long, lingering hug.

She needs my hand as we walk at her pace.
He needs to hear he's doing just fine.
She needs to know it's okay to fall down.
He needs my acceptance.
She needs my guidance.
He needs to know that hearing about his day is the best part of my day.

And what do *I* need? I need to breathe. I need to laugh. I need to take time to love and be loved.

In the flurry and frenzy of our busy lives, our inherent needs get covered up. Our most vital needs get buried beneath extraneous needs, immediate needs, and superficial needs.

But the needs that keep spirits alive, nourish souls, strengthen bonds, and build futures are the needs that must not be forgotten in the blur of a frenzied day.

He needs love.
She needs love.
I need love.
We have the power to fulfill those needs.
Today, let us give love where it's needed most.

Today's Reminder

Within each day of my busy life, the most critical needs often get buried beneath non-essential needs. But the needs that keep spirits alive, strengthen bonds, and build promising futures are the needs that must not be forgotten. He needs love. She needs love. I need love. *I have the power to fulfill that need by asking this critical question: "What do they really need?" Today I will seek to fulfill true needs rather than superficial needs. I look forward to seeing what goodness unfolds as a result.*

30

AWARENESS

On a glorious Saturday, I bought some
time. It wasn't free,
but the cost was small in comparison to
what I gained.

BUY SOME TIME

You can buy a yellow flowerpot, a bottle of water, or a snazzy pair of shoes. We all know that. But rarely do we think about buying time.

Well, the other day, I did that—I bought some time.

It was a Saturday—a glorious Saturday—the kind of day that causes regret if you don't get outside and enjoy at least some part of it, like coming home from the fair with a ticket in your pocket, like wasting something of value, like missing your chance for the big prize.

So on this glorious Saturday, I decided not to waste that ticket in my pocket. And with it, I bought some time. Of course, it wasn't free.

It cost me one no to an outside request.
It cost me a load of laundry that didn't get folded.
It cost me a delay in cleaning the kitchen.
It cost me an opportunity to corral the family to all the places we could go.

It cost me a missed phone call and a handful of texts.

It cost me some angst—the feeling that I should really be doing something productive—but I quickly got over that.

I used that ticket to say yes to hiking up a mountain with my family. I ended up getting much more than I bargained for . . .

I got some fresh air.
I got some blood pressure relief.
I got some insight into my loved ones' hearts and minds.
I got some memories to comfort me in my later years.
I got a laugh . . . or two . . . or three. I lost count.
I got a spark of life back in my weary bones.

But the real prize came after we ate our picnic at the top of that mountain. I stretched out on a slab of rock in the sun. The next thing I knew, there was one daughter on each side of me with no space in between our bodies.

That's when my younger daughter turned and looked straight into my soul. She said, "This is the life, Mama."

What my contented heart heard was, "This is the *Life Mama*."

Learning when to say no to the things that cluttered, suffocated, and distracted me from what mattered most provided oxygen to my soul. Learning when to say yes to what mattered most brought me back to life.

On a glorious Saturday, I bought some time. It wasn't free. But the cost was small in comparison to what I gained.

That evening I walked down a mountain with tired legs and a revitalized heart. I was the one with the biggest smile.

Today's Reminder

Today I will be asked to do many things. Some requests will be non-negotiable; others will be a choice. In deciding which requests to fulfill, I will remember I have a right to protect family time and life fulfillment time. No one is going to protect it for me. Today I might decide to buy some time. Even a few minutes of breathing room is enough to bring love where it's desperately needed and peace to my frenzied soul.

31

Gratitude

It might be a hard Monday, but it's a new day,
and here you are, in all your glory.

FINDING GLORY

It might be a hard Monday, but it's a new day.
It might be a half-hearted hug, but it's better than an angry good-bye.
It might be a grouchy face, but it's been covered in your kisses since day one.
It might be a soft, imperfect body, but it's done a good job of housing your beating heart.
It might be a small step, but it's going forward.
It might be a failed attempt, but it's better than no attempt at all.

It might be over too soon, but it was fun while it lasted.
It might be only a short break, but it's still a breather.
It might be a boring old sandwich, but it's sustenance, and it's made with love.
It might be a long road ahead, but it's heading toward the light.
It might not be going so well, but it's not over yet.
It might not be your moment of glory, but there's glory in the moments . . .
Glory in the grouchy face that softens with a kiss.
Glory in the tender flesh around your hopeful heart.
Glory in the small steps forward made by courageous feet.
Glory in the fact that you keep showing up, even when it's hard.
It might be a hard Monday, but it's a new day,
and here you are, in all your glory.

Today's Reminder

I refuse to waste any more time cataloging my gripes and grievances. Instead, I want to keep track of what is good and holy and helpful and true. Once my eyes begin to notice life's ripe fruits, I can't help but look for more. Today I will live by this motto: "Here I am in all my glory, looking for my glory moments!"

32

Gratitude

Today I lived.
It wasn't my first response,
but I share the same heartbeat with two precious souls,
and that's enough to get me through the day.

LOVE WASN'T MY FIRST RESPONSE

I was on a mission to tuck my daughter into bed as quickly as possible. It had been a tiring day, and I just wanted to be alone.

She asked if she could listen to my heartbeat.

Reluctantly I cuddled up next to her, and she rested her head on my chest. "We have the same heartbeat," she announced.

"How do you know?" I asked, expecting some childlike reasoning, but instead her poignant response brought me to my knees.

"Because you are my mom."
There it was. My confirmation.
To choose to stay when I want to retreat.
To choose to forgive when I want to condemn.
To choose to love when I want to attack.
To choose to hope when I want to doubt.
To choose to stand when I want to fall.
Today I loved.
It wasn't my first response,
but I share the same heartbeat with two precious souls,
and that's enough to get me through the day.
I will choose to love again tomorrow.

Today's Reminder

Today I will ask my loved ones if I can do the "heartbeat check." I will lay my head on their chests and describe what I hear. This loving action might bring giggles, or conversation, or stillness. I won't know the result until I try. But one thing for certain: the "heartbeat check" offers solace. No matter how crazy the day, no matter how discouraged I feel, no matter how dismal the state of our world, the heartbeat check offers refuge. There is nothing more hopeful than the sound of the human heart—especially when it belongs to someone I love more than life.

33

Gratitude

Let's not look to inanimate things with no voice,
no pulse, and no soul to find life's goodness.
Life's goodness is right here—being, breathing,
and blossoming right in front of our eyes.

PUMPING LIFE'S GOODNESS INTO OUR VEINS

Looking for a sign of life? Just watch her face light up when she sees you; that'll get your heart pumping.

Straining for the sound of joy? Just listen for the giggles when his favorite part comes up; prepare to tickle your senses.

Searching for a little hope? Just place your ear against her beating heart; you'll find peace has a rhythm.

Waiting for the sun to come out? Just grasp his hand; therein lies the warmth of a million suns.

Hoping for a brighter future? Just watch the excitement bubble over when you say, "Tell me your dream, child." That'll revive your dying ambition.

Today let's not look to inanimate things with no voice, no pulse, and no soul to find life's goodness.

Life's goodness is right here.
It's right here, standing in front of us,
breathing and being and blossoming
before our eyes.

It's easy to get sidetracked
by this world with its pace and its waste and its weight
always pulling us away.
But not today. Today we are back in focus.
Ear to heart,
hand in hand,
eyes wide open,
arms outstretched,
life's goodness pumping into our veins.

Today's Reminder

The time I spend staring at screens, juggling packed agendas, and managing life's endless duties takes an unseen toll. I must remember the healing power of eye contact, touch, and real conversation—the stuff that makes me happy to be alive. Today I will push aside life's distractions and make at least one soul-to-soul connection. Today I will look longer and more completely into the eyes of those I love. Today I will see the goodness standing right in front of me.

34

Grace

The glorious offering of this day:
a chance to love and be loved,
a chance to live and let live,
a reason to celebrate,
a time to breathe,
a shot at peace,
one less regret tomorrow.

TODAY'S GLORIOUS OFFERINGS

Today I might have too many things on my plate, but I will remember I don't have to do them all.

Today I might have too many balls in the air, but I will remember to catch the most important ones.

Today might be one mad dash from morning to night, but I will remember my people cannot kiss a moving target—and I'll stop for love. I'll stop for love.

Today I might feel like I am going nowhere, but I will remember how far I've come.

Today I might have my patience tested, but I will remember the saving grace of a three-second pause.

Today I might mess up many times, but I will remember I'm the only one keeping track. *Only Love Today. Only Love Today.*

Today I might not see the blessings beneath the mess and mayhem of my life, but I will remember to keep looking.

Today I will try to remember the glorious offerings of
this day:
a chance to love and be loved,
a chance to live and let live,
a reason to celebrate,
a time to breathe,
a shot at peace,
and one less regret tomorrow.

Today's Reminder

Today I will not collapse in utter exhaustion without having one significant memory to cherish because I chose to be too busy, too annoyed, too distracted, and too focused on perfection and productivity to recognize and appreciate the blessings in my life. Today my goal for my family is this: to gather together with our messy, flawed human hearts in hopes of making happy memories that will outlast us all.

35

GRACE

I know these actions are more than just actions, because I put love in them.

MORE THAN JUST ACTIONS

Sometimes when I make a simple meal,
served up hot,
I ask, "How does it taste, love?" as they gobble it up.
I grab that moment,
and I savor it.

It's probably not someone else's idea of a "shining moment,"
but it's mine.

Because you see, I do this every day,
this showing up even when I don't feel like it,
to provide a warm meal,
a warm embrace,
a warm assurance,
a warm blanket,
a warm hand.
I know these actions are more than just actions because
I put love in them.

That's probably why I find myself calling my people "love" sometimes.

That's what I feel in that moment—my shining moment—when love stares back at me, bringing light to the darkest fabric of my days.

Today's Reminder

Today I vow to lower the bar on what makes me a good parent, spouse, caregiver, friend, or human being. Because the truth is this: It's not the grand gestures, the beautiful presentations, or the flawless execution of my tasks that nourish and nurture my people. It's the love—the love I serve up day in and day out, no matter what challenges we face. So today if I'm bringing the love, I'll remember I'm doing just fine.

36

Gratitude

What if the most coveted gifts were ones that cost nothing but a little time and presence?

PEOPLE WHO LIKE TO HELP

My family had the opportunity to redecorate a dismal, dark room at a local women's shelter. As my children cleaned, organized, and rearranged, I was struck by the number of residents who stopped to say, "Thank you for being here." But there was one comment from a shelter resident that will undoubtedly stick with me forever.

After watching the children fold baby clothes into tiny stacks, this woman said, "You like to help people, don't you? I can tell."

In a society where grand achievements and small waistlines
are complimented on a daily basis,
in a world where "busy" is a badge of honor and excess is
the norm,
in a time when electronic messages are chosen over face-to-
face contact,
this compliment got me thinking.
What if emphasis was placed not on the value of our home,
but on the openness of our hands?
What if the warmth of our smile was noticed over the
whiteness of our teeth?
What if the most coveted gifts were ones that cost nothing
but a little time and presence?
Well, if the day we spent at the women's shelter is any
indication, this would mean . . .
less competition, more compassion;
less greed, more gratitude;
less putting each other down, more holding each other up.

So today I will be looking—looking for those with warm smiles, helpful hands, and generous hearts. Today I will be looking for People Who Like to Help.

They may never make the cover of a magazine, but they make the world a better place.

I plan to tell them so.

Today's Reminder

This week I will designate a day for expressing love to special people outside our family's circle—those whose helpful efforts often go unseen or unappreciated. I will prepare a small treat and add a kind note. I will hand it to them in the checkout line. I'll leave it in the mailbox or on the trash bin. I'll place it on their desks or give it to them in person. I will say, "I really appreciate you." It doesn't take much to make someone's day. It doesn't take much to create a sense of hope in the world. It doesn't take much to turn an average day into a memorable one.

37

GRACE

When you can't see the goodness through
the chaos and the clutter,
remember to keep looking.

KEEP LOOKING

When the toilet overflows, remember to breathe.
When the news is too bleak, remember to hope.
When harsh words are about to come out, remember to pause.
Even a brief pause can do wonders.

When your feet get too weary, remember to dance.
When you feel like you don't have enough, remember to give.
When you fear you've done too much damage, remember you've got today to make amends.
Even a quiet "I'm sorry" can do wonders.

When you feel like you're going nowhere, remember how far you've come.
When you feel like a colossal failure, remember you are your worst critic.
When you're just too tired, remember it's okay to stop.
Even a brief rest can do wonders.

When you have too many steps to take, remember tiny efforts count.
When you see too much darkness ahead, remember love lights the path.
When the morning is one mad dash, remember to say good-bye.
Even a brief hug can do wonders.

When you can't see the goodness through the chaos and the clutter, remember to keep looking.
The moments that keep us going can be found in the most unexpected places, in the most challenging times. Even just one of them, tucked inside the heart and mind of our precious one in the midst of a trying day, can do wonders.

Today's Reminder

Today I will remember the power of one. If I'm feeling overwhelmed by the tasks or duties ahead of me, I will remind myself I do not have to do them all at once; I just need to start with one. I will get into the habit of asking, What matters most right now? *Making what matters most my reference point will consistently steer me back to a positive direction, no matter how far off the path I've gotten.*

— IV —

Winter: Holding On

Hope, Encouragement, and Introspection

In the face of challenge and uncertainty, sometimes the best thing you can do is just hold on.

"We are all ready," Natalie messaged me with a picture of two smiling, early-morning faces. Days before, she'd assured me she and her sister didn't need anyone to care for them when Scott and I left at five o'clock in the morning to go to the hospital for my third surgery. She assured me she could get them up, fed, and ready for school by seven o'clock. I had faith in them; I said okay. Like any good Type-A list maker would, I left a checklist for my firstborn child, being sure to mention the importance of waking her little sister up *gently*.

So there I was, garbed in my surgical gown and ghastly cap—teeth chattering, no less. But instead of worrying about my impending surgery, I thought about how things were going at home. Would the kids get themselves off to school okay?

With one message and one photo, my question was answered. One big, fat tear ran down my cheek. They could do it. They could do it. What a beautiful answer I'd just received.

Shortly after I received Natalie's uplifting text message, I was wheeled into the operating room. I was greeted with cold air and lively music. I was usually good at "Name That Tune," but for some reason, I couldn't remember the title of that familiar song. I knew I liked it, though. It was a good dance song.

"I forgot you played music in the operating room!" I said excitedly to the nurse, as if we were walking into a club. Music is my thing. It often serves as my warm blanket in trying times. I couldn't believe I'd forgotten about this little operating room "perk."

"Some patients don't like it," the nurse said, "but many do."

"Well, I love it," I said enthusiastically, hoping she'd crank up the volume. Instead she instructed me to transfer myself from the bed to the operating table. I knew exactly how to do it. I felt like a pro.

Within minutes the anesthesiologist was giving me information, and I felt a cool rush in my IV.

"It's too tight on my arm," I said in a shaky voice that felt like it might crack.

"It's because I gave you some medicine. Don't worry. We'll take good care of you." Her voice was calm.

I immediately thought about the confusion regarding my surgical order. One order said *right cystoscopy*, and the other said something about a procedure on the left. Several medical personnel had gathered around the papers, trying to decipher them. The nurses ended up putting bands scribbled with instructions in black Sharpie on both my arms. They assured me they knew what they were doing on each side, but I felt uncertain.

That's when my favorite song by Train came on the radio. Pat Monahan's soulful voice filled the room, describing the comfort found in the heavens above during times of struggle.

All at once, I felt God's unmistakable presence assuring me things would be okay. The doctor would do what was needed on the appropriate side of my body, and I would wake up with more time to love and be loved. What a beautiful answer.

When I got home from the hospital, I pulled out my special "good luck" surgery box from Natalie. It contained new pajamas, fuzzy socks, and two little notebooks for jotting down my thoughts. I covered myself in a new electric blanket sent by a dear friend. I held on to an inspirational quote booklet handmade by another friend. But it wasn't until I clicked on the bedside lamp that I fully realized the momentousness of this occasion. I was home! I was alive! Had the medical team uncovered the reason for my ongoing pain or hydronephrosis (kidney swelling)? No, they had not. Was there a plan in place? No, there was not. Did I have any idea what I would do next? No, I did not. *But I was not without answers.* My grateful heart nearly overflowed with answers of the most precious kind.

I took out one of the little notebooks Natalie had tucked inside my care package and wrote this:

Sometimes you don't get the answers you're hoping for.
Instead, you get different ones.
And they're better than you could ever imagine.

I sent a message to my dearest friends, letting them know I was okay but hadn't gotten the answers I was seeking. I wrote, "Going to just sit with that for a bit and figure my next step in time. My body and mind have been through a lot, and I just need some time to collect myself."

My friend Kerry responded with this: "I like how you worded your reaction to no news. My gut reaction is to send you words of comfort to try and 'fix' it for you. But I won't. I, too, will sit with the words from your doctor."

That's when I remembered something I'd written almost a year ago. I opened my laptop and searched my files for the phrase "sit with it awhile." As I tearfully read the piece that pulled up, I felt like I was reading a "note to self." But I was pretty sure it wasn't just for me. It was a note to multiple selves, those facing questions without answers. This is what my note to self said:

Maybe the best thing you could do right now is just sit with it awhile.

Maybe the bravest thing you could do right now is just decide this will not defeat you.

Maybe the most productive thing you could do right now is just fold your hands in prayerful silence.

Maybe the most sensible thing you could do right now is just laugh . . . laugh in the face of it all.

Maybe the most powerful thing you could do right now is just close your eyes and envision a positive outcome.

Maybe the most loving thing you could do right now is just give yourself room to breathe.

Maybe the best thing to do right now looks like nothing at all.

But it's not.

Because when you're gathering hope, it's patient.

When you're gathering strength, it's quiet.

When you're gathering resilience, it's unnoticeable.

In the face of challenge and uncertainty,

sometimes the best thing you can do right now is just hold on.

From where I rested comfortably in my bed, I could clearly see all the things I'd learned from my ongoing medical trial. I learned we must not ignore our bodies. I learned we must not go through our struggles alone—we must let someone in. I learned we are worthy of self-care, just as we give care to our loved ones. I learned we need to get to the bottom of persistent and mysterious pains, because if we don't, who will? I learned quiet prayers and small acts of kindness hold great power.

Those were the obvious things I learned. But that day, in the uncomfortable space between answers, I was able to see one more truth—a not-so-obvious truth I wouldn't have grasped had I not allowed myself to rest in a heavenly place of surrender.

That life-changing truth was this: *just because we stop fighting, searching, plotting, planning, and thinking about it today doesn't mean we're giving up forever.*

Today might be a day to sit with it.
Today might be a day to collect yourself.
Today might be a day to cuddle with a blanket and soak up the love being given to you.
Today might be a day not to think about tomorrow.
Today might be a day to simply *be*, and that is enough.

Perhaps you find yourself in an uncomfortable place today. Perhaps the pain is so close to home you don't know what to do. Perhaps uncertainty hovers over you like a dark cloud. Perhaps the hope muscles are tired; the smile is strained. Perhaps the "it'll be okay" is starting to sound hollow. Perhaps you are worried—worried about yourself, your loved ones, or the state of the world. Perhaps you are wondering if you will ever have the answers you need to move forward.

Just stop for a moment and listen. Perhaps your heart has been longing to hear these words:

Today is not a day of action—it is a day of resting, breathing, pausing, and praying.

Dear one, you don't have to have the answers today. Today is your day of surrender, of holding on and being held in God's mighty hands. If you don't think relinquishment is possible for your active body, mind, and soul, read on. The season ahead is life's intermission, a chance to breathe and restore. Each entry you'll encounter is an encouraging *note to self*, cultivating quiet strength, introspection, and hope. Through each reading, you'll gain permission to "sit with it," to listen, to trust, to surrender.

Today you are triumphantly holding on. You are quietly gathering hope. And that is enough. It is more than enough. By choosing to rest in this place of uncertainty, answers to your heart's most important questions will be revealed. Stop. Breathe. Hold on as you are being held.

1

Hope

This life you didn't necessarily plan for is
becoming quite beautiful on you.

IN THE LIGHT OF THE UNEXPECTED

It might be that day of the week,
or that particular season,
or that darkest hour
when you've come to the end of your rope;
when your dreams seem impossibly far away,
when nothing seems to fit in its proper place,
when the bedcovers look like an inviting place to stay forever.
"This is not what I expected," you might say
on this day of the week,
in this particular season,
of your darkest hour.
That's okay.
That's okay.
It doesn't mean it can't work out, or be okay,
or become something better than you expected in time.
Just because it's not what you expected doesn't mean it's turning out all wrong.
Each time you
open your arms,
pick your battles,
breathe through the meltdowns,

work through the upheavals,
spot the silver linings,
carry the weight that's too big to be carried,
it becomes you.
It becomes you.
This life you didn't necessarily plan for is becoming quite beautiful on you.
In these diversions from the path you imagined, expected, or hoped for,
there are opportunities to see the silver linings of your soul you didn't even know you had.
But now you do. Now you do.
Shine on, dear one. You radiate strength in the light of the unexpected.

Today's Reminder

Uncertainty and change can be difficult and stressful. I often put pressure on myself to have every situation resolved quickly and every blank filled in completely, but I'm finding there is divine peace in acknowledging I don't have to have it all figured out. By surrendering, my worry eases, and the empty spaces are filled in better ways than I could have imagined. Today I will surrender my empty spaces, and I'll offer the same peace to my loved ones. I trust things will work out in time; I can let go of the problem for now, knowing I am held in God's loving hands.

2

Encouragement

When faced with personal challenges and life issues, let us remember someone is listening, and the words we choose may be the message that someone has been waiting to hear.

THE WORDS WE CHOOSE

"I love myself," she heard her mother say.

"I didn't do as well as I hoped, but I'll keep trying," he heard his father say.

"My pants are a little tight around the waist, but I am not going to let it stop me from having fun with the family today," she heard her sister say.

"I'm not going to judge. Everyone does things a little differently, and that's okay," he heard his uncle say.

"It's not perfect, but it's good enough for today," she heard her teacher say.

"I could worry about it, but I choose to focus my energies on what I can control," he heard his grandmother say.

"I forgive myself for the mistakes of the past," she heard her friend say.

"I am going to ask for help. It's brave to ask for help," he heard his grandfather say.

When faced with personal challenges and life issues, let us remember,
self-kindness is contagious,
compassion spreads,
acceptance empowers.
One positive thought spoken out loud has the potential to become
someone's day changer,
someone's game changer,
someone's perspective changer.
When faced with personal challenges and life issues, let us remember someone is listening,

and the words we choose may be the message that someone has been waiting to hear.
They could be a life changer.

Today's Reminder

No matter what role I play, I can offer hope to others by offering compassion to myself. What message do I want my loved ones to speak to themselves? I will start speaking those messages to myself. I will speak them loud enough to create a ripple of positivity with endless possibilities.

3

Encouragement

Just hold out your hands; the offering to give love is also a chance to be loved.

LOVE IS HOW YOU ROLL

Bags under your eyes?
No problem.
Just rest them on a face that loves you.
She doesn't see dark circles—she only notices the way they light up when her laugh comes straight from her belly.

Pants too tight?
No problem.
Just allow your favorite pair of arms to enclose you.
Those arms don't feel a size—they feel home.

Overwhelmed with regret?
No problem.
Just go and tuck those soft covers around your beloved.
He doesn't care how many times you've fallen down; he only sees that you're standing here now.

Feeling less than shiny and put together?
No problem.
Let down your hair, and turn up your favorite song.
Your dancing partner doesn't see ugliness; he sees the life of his party.

Feeling unlovable?
No problem.
Just hold out your hands.
The offering to give love is also a chance to be loved.

Before you scrutinize,
tear down,
or judge yourself with critical eyes,
think about what you offer up every day to the people who share your life: love.
Love is how you roll.
So today, give a little of that love to yourself.

Today's Reminder

No matter how my body looks today, it's served me well. It's housed my beating heart all these years, and that is truly significant! Today I will treat my body with the love and respect it deserves. I will not stand in front of the mirror deciding whether I am fit for public observation. I will not throw another outfit to my closet floor, taking shreds of my dignity with it. I will not apologize for the space I inhabit. I am worthy of love. My body is worthy of love without conditions and restraint.

4

Hope

If you find it hard to hold on, do it anyway.
You may look down and see someone holding
on simply because you are.

DO IT ANYWAY

If you find it hard to get up,
do it anyway.
You may see someone brighten at the mere sight of you.

If you find it hard to look at your reflection,
do it anyway.
You may see a flicker of something beautiful you thought was gone.

If you find it hard to love the unlovable,
do it anyway.
You may see a smile or an expression that reminds you of their worth.

If you find it hard to get past the mess,
do it anyway.
You may see evidence of precious hands learning, loving, and living.

If you find it hard to speak out,
do it anyway.
You may have the words someone else needs to hear.

If you find it hard to hold on,
do it anyway.
You may look down and see someone holding on
simply because you are.

Today's Reminder

Today I release myself from pain and insecurity. I will no longer let debilitating feelings dictate my life. I will no longer let them stop me from doing what my heart longs to do. I might only be able to stand for five minutes. I might have shaky hands. I might speak in a whisper, but I will create. I will shine. I will live.

5

Introspection

A little more time can be a miraculous thing.

I AM NOT READY

"Do I have to rush?" my child asked worriedly as she sat down to enjoy a heaping snow cone.

For once I said the words that almost never passed my lips. "Just take your time, baby. You don't have to rush."

Her little shoulders relaxed; she exhaled; her face radiated joy. I had given her the gift of time. That moment made an impression on me. *Perhaps there are words that can undo the damage of a hurried life,* I thought optimistically. And so I kept trying to give that child the gift of time as she grew.

I learned to wake her up gently, giving her time to stretch and adjust to the light.

I learned to give her five minutes to pick out and put on her pajamas. Those extra minutes gave her time to inhale the clean smell that made her so happy.

I learned to count to twenty in my head as she carefully sprinkled cinnamon on her applesauce. She said it tasted better that way, and her smile told me that it really did.

I learned to notice her expression when she was scared to try something new. I learned when she needed to hear, "Maybe not today," or "Two seconds of bravery is all it takes! You can do this!"

It was apparent these offerings of time were a gift to my child, yet I had a feeling there was something more.

I recently figured out what that "something more" was. It dawned on me when I heard a little voice inside me whisper, "I am not ready."

For the first time, I didn't push the voice away. I didn't ignore it. I didn't power through.

I listened. I gave myself a few more days. I gave myself a break instead of a deadline. I actually crawled back into bed, something I hadn't done since I was very sick in high school.

Here I am today, feeling so much better. Feeling courage I didn't have last week. Feeling a sense of hope that eluded me days ago. Feeling clear and not fuzzy. My delay was not a waste; it was a gift to myself.

It made me think of you, dear one, living in a culture where efficiency, productivity, and perfection are constantly tapping us on the shoulder.

Pausing, delaying, and waiting are not recommended in this fast-paced world where we are pressured to do everything now, not later. In light of that, I thought I'd pass a refreshing idea on to you.

To you, the one not ready to move on,
and to you, the one not ready to let go.

To you, the one not ready to step up to the plate
and the one not ready to call it quits.

To the one not ready to try again,
the one not ready to give up,

the one not ready to bow out,
and the one not ready to get over it.

To you, the one not ready to pick herself up
and to you, the one not ready to back down.

To you, the one not ready to go there
and the one not ready to put one foot in front of the other.

I hear you.
I hear you.
You are not ready today,
and it's okay.
It's okay.
Just because you're not ready today doesn't mean you won't be ready tomorrow, or in a few days, or ever.
Just because you are not ready today doesn't mean you are weak or selfish or lazy.

Just because the world is always so go, go, go
and so quick to judge
and so eager to move you forward,
doesn't mean you can't stay here, right where you are, for a bit
until you decide for yourself that you're ready.

Because the world that thinks it knows so much
doesn't know what is best for you.

But your heart does. Your heart knows what's best for you.

If that little voice inside you is saying, "I'm not ready,"
then listen.
Just listen. And wait.
The time will come.

Today's Reminder

Today I will give the gift of time—to my loved one, my coworker, the cashier working so hard. I will notice the relief in her eyes and the exhale when I say, "Take your time." I will also give the gift of time to myself at least once today. I will see how a moment sheltered from the rush and pressures of daily life can become a moment of connection, redemption, trust, or peace. A little more time can be a miraculous thing.

6

Hope

I see you're having a bad day today. I have them too. I won't give up on you.

I Can Take It

Upon learning that a certain precious nursing home resident we knew never had any visitors, Avery said, "We can be her family, Mama!" So for several months, we visited Annie and gathered small details from the staff about what she loved most. We were warned that sometimes Annie got confused and upset, but we never experienced anything other than a sweet and cooperative woman who loved Elvis Presley, arts and crafts, and being outside.

One day my daughter became worried that Annie might forget her since it had been more than a week since our last visit. When we arrived at the nursing home, we were surprised and saddened to find Annie hunched over and despondent in her wheelchair. When we said hello, we did not receive the usual cheerful greeting. It hurt my heart to see Annie like this, and for a moment I thought maybe we should go. But Avery stepped forward and told Annie she'd learned her favorite Elvis song and wanted to sing it to her. That's when Annie said, "Okay," instead of "What do you want?"

We took Annie outside to her favorite spot by the fountain. Avery kneeled down in front of her friend and sang, "Fools Rush In" and "You Are My Sunshine." Annie perked up for a brief moment and sang along softly. We thought she might enjoy some painting, but she grabbed her arm in agony shortly after she began. Annie asked Avery to finish her picture and then sat quietly staring at her lap. When it was time to go, Avery said, "I love you. We'll be back again soon!"

My child never said a word about the difference in Annie that day, but it wasn't because she didn't notice—my little girl notices everything. I honestly think it was because when she said, "We can be her family," she meant it. To my daughter, being family means not giving up on each other; it means not withholding the love that's in your heart, even when the other person is having a bad day.

Although it appeared Annie was not fully present for our visit, something tells me she received the exact message she needed that day. I think it's a message worth sharing, because sometime we'll all need this message—either as the giver or the receiver. Feel free to use it as you see fit:

"I see you're having a bad day today. I know. I have them too. But I won't give up on you. We'll do the things you like to do. I'll sing to you. I'll hold the paintbrush when your arm hurts. Or we can just sit together quietly and watch the birds. You don't have to talk. I know you aren't yourself today. It's okay. I can take it. I love you."

TODAY'S REMINDER

Each time I pour love into someone or something, I am making a priceless investment. Such a selfless act can feel depleting, exhausting, and at times unreciprocated. Investing love into the life of another is not always easy, but let me not forget why I do it: Love makes good things possible. *Today I will keep giving my love away. It might just find its way back to me when I least expect it but need it the most.*

7

ENCOURAGEMENT

By receiving each other with acceptance,
grace, and unconditional love,
we can bring each other home.

WHAT WE ALL WANT TO KNOW

All fifth grade parents were invited to an informational meeting at the middle school our children would be attending in the fall. After greeting the parents seated around me, I settled in to absorb everything I could about helping my daughter make a smooth transition from elementary school to sixth grade. But I received something more. I received something that has helped me connect better with my child and with every single person I encounter. It has even helped me respond better to myself.

The assistant principal said this: "You might think opening their locker or having seven teachers is the greatest worry for sixth graders on that first day of school—but it's not. In general, their biggest source of angst is knowing how they're getting home."

The administrator proceeded to explain where bus routes could be accessed during the summer months, but I was only half listening. All I could think about was this:

They just want to know how they're getting home.

Isn't that what we all really want?

To know, at the end of the day, there will be a welcoming smile and two open arms waiting for us, no matter what we've done, no matter what kind of day we've had.

Today someone you love might be over-the-top dramatic.
Someone might be unusually clingy.
Someone might have a lot of questions or some extra hostility.
Someone might be quiet and withdrawn.
Someone might be cloaked in worry.
Someone might have paper-thin patience.
Before you respond, take a moment to remember this:
He just wants to know how he's getting home.
She just wants to know how she's getting home.
And you do too.
Whether we wear a smile or not,
whether we have our ducks in a row or they are running loose,
whether we know what the future holds or have no clue,
whether we are standing on solid ground or sinking sand,
we all share one commonality:
we just want to know how we're getting home.
And we can get there, my friend. We can get there.
By receiving each other with acceptance, grace, and unconditional love,
we can bring each other home.

Today's Reminder

Today I will try to remember that everyone I encounter has something weighing down his or her soul. Perhaps I will be able to tell by their attitudes or facial expressions. Perhaps I will not be able to tell at all. But it will serve me well to remember that person has a beating heart just like mine—and today it might be in pain. Whether it's a young person, a grown person, or even myself; a little more patience, a little more kindness, and a little more compassion can go a long way.

8

Introspection

Today when I look at you, I will try to focus
on what's more than okay in both of us.

WHAT'S MORE THAN OKAY

I look at you and see the damage.
"That's me," I say when my not-so-desirable qualities
surface in you.
I'm too impatient.
I'm too controlling.
I'm a worrywart.

I'm too independent,
too headstrong,
too overreactive,
too stubborn,
too sensitive,

too head-in-the-clouds.

I am afraid I've passed it all down to you.
I'm afraid it's beyond repair.

Then I see you hold a puppy,
take the lead,
write a story,
run with your hair flying,
create like an artist,
laugh with your mouth wide open,
protect your sister,
wipe another's tears,
come up with a plan.

I say, "That's me," and perhaps I am not a complete mess.
There's some good in there.
And you're picking up on that,
along with your own unique strengths, talents, and gifts.

For the first time, I feel hopeful
that my not-so-desirable qualities can soften over time;
that my rough edges can smooth out with each passing day.

And maybe I'm more okay than I thought I was.
Maybe you'll be okay too.
Maybe you already are.

Today when I look at you, I will try to focus on what's more
    than okay
in both of us.

Today's Reminder

Today I will ask my loved ones two very important questions: "What's your dream?" and "What do you want to be?" No matter what they say, I will not laugh. I will not judge. I will not dissuade. There is no wrong answer to this question. After noticing the hope and excitement in my loved ones' eyes and voices when they share their dreams, I will ask one more very important question: "How can I support your dream?" For both the dreamer, and the one who supports him, hope is abundant.

9

Introspection

The more I looked for joy in unexpected moments, the more it came around.

COME BACK, JOY

Peace left my house without so much as a good-bye.
I haven't seen Patience in quite some time.
Stillness doesn't come around much anymore. It's always go-go-go 'round here.
Hope is scarce.
Self-love is a stranger.
Enthusiasm has gone and left me spiritless.
Courage is missing.
Focus has completely abandoned me.
I think I'll put up a sign the way people do for lost pets.
"Come back, Joy," it will read.
Come back, Gratitude.
Come back, Energy.

Come back, Zest.
I'm looking for you,
and I won't stop until I find you
because life's just not the same without you.

I remember the day I realized the smile had permanently left my face. Acknowledging I'd become a negative person was painful, but it was an essential step to finding my joy again. I vowed to look for the flowers instead of the weeds in people and situations. I found unexpected joy in a love note from my younger daughter, so I taped it to the kitchen cabinet. I taped another one of her notes on my closet door, and then one on the bathroom mirror. These signs reminded me to keep looking for joy. I found it in the smell of my husband's aftershave when I hugged him, so I breathed it in. I found it in my older daughter making muffins, so I joined her. I found it in my own poetic scribbles, so I wrote a little bit each day. The more I looked for joy in unexpected moments, the more it came around. Now I think it's here to stay.

Today's Reminder

What's missing from my heart? What's missing from my life? I will invite what's missing to come back by writing it down on a piece of paper and posting it in a prominent place. Then I will be on the lookout. I will look for what is missing with all my might. Even a brief glimpse of it will inspire hope that more goodness is waiting around the bend.

10

Encouragement

There are just some things that
should not be faced alone.

AT THE BOTTOM OF THE BOAT

It's hard to hold your own hand.
It's hard to lean on your own shoulder.
It's hard to see the parade without someone boosting you up.

It's hard to pat your own back.
It's hard to see the light when you are lost in the darkest part of your forest.
It's hard to bail water out of your own sinking boat.

And because there are just some things that should not be faced alone, I believe this:
Maybe the answer to someone else's troubling situation is not to fix it,
or have all the answers,
but to simply sit beside them
and say, "If your boat is going down, I am going down with you."

And when he is not so busy trying to figure out how to hold his own hand
(because you are holding it)
and when she stops wasting so much energy trying to find a map out of darkness
(because she is using your perspective)
they might have the ability to spot an oar at the bottom of the boat
they didn't see before.
Together we can keep each other afloat.

Today's Reminder

It's difficult to see my loved ones suffer. I can't fix their problems. I can't take away their pain. But all hope is not lost. I can offer my presence. I can be a constant in a period of upheaval. I can say, "We don't have to talk right now, but I'd love to sit beside you." Today I will make myself available so that when my loved one is ready to talk, I will be there to listen. When faced with disappointment or feelings of inadequacy, my loved ones need my presence more than my words.

11

Hope

Today I stop worrying so much about
what could happen *to our children*
and instead focus on what they could make happen.

FIX IT UP FOR GOOD

There's nothing I'd like to do more than fix up the world for you.
To extinguish the hate.
To dismantle the bombs.
To clean up the sad state of affairs.
To expose the danger hidden in broad daylight.

There's nothing I'd like to do more than fix up the world for you.
To mend what's broken.
To save what's drowning.

To preserve what's dying.
To heal what's hurting.

I've thought a lot about this. I've worried about your future. I've worried about your safety. I've wondered if there's any hope left in the world.

Then I saw you waiting for Grandpa. He was moving very slowly. You smiled as if to say, "Take your time."

Later you said, "Today I waited for Grandpa. That's what Noticers do. They notice what is needed. Grandpa needed me to wait."

Suddenly, it all seemed very clear. I will not cover my eyes when I watch the news and see the state of the world. Instead, I will set my eyes on the children before me:

the Noticers,
the Dreamers,
the Seat Savers,
the Doodlers,
the Energizers,
the Difference Makers,
the Believers,
the Song Writers,
the Flower Sniffers,
the Toothless Smilers,
the Fearless Leaders,
the Hand Holders,
the Hand Raisers,
the Defenders.

I no longer wonder if there's any hope left in the world. I know there is. It is inside my child's beating heart. Today is the day I stop worrying so much about what *could happen* to our children and instead focus on what they *could make happen*. They could bring what is needed to the world and fix it up for good.

Today's Reminder

Today I will gather my loved ones and ask them how we could bring goodness to the world. Maybe we will make cards or cookies. Maybe we will hold doors or pick up trash. Maybe we will visit a nursing home, fire station, or homeless shelter. With every human story that is changed for good, there is one less story of hate, violence, greed, and animosity. With every life touched, the world becomes a better place. Our hands hold the hope this world needs.

12

Hope

When you have the most important things in life—love, faith, and family—there is nothing you own that you can't give away.

A Piece of Fruit

My child has always gravitated toward the world's suffering, has always been one to want to know the world in its truest state. Starting when Natalie was very small, the recurring question at bedtime was always, "Mama, tell me something bad that happened in the news today."

With reluctance, I explained in words she could understand about the atrocities many people faced, the dangers that lurked, and those who'd lost so much. Then I stood by and watched her digest every troubling morsel I offered. Time after time, I worried that it was too much, too overwhelming, too disturbing. After all, the problems of the world are vast and insurmountable. At least that is what I used to think.

Thanks to the heart of a child, now I know differently.

One day when we drove into the city, Natalie saw with her own two eyes the world her mother spoke of—the one that could be cruel, hungry, desperate, and cold.

But she was not scared.

Oh no, she had been waiting for this moment, dreaming of this moment, when she could do something to help.

You see, her eight-year-old eyes did not look at the scene and see daunting global issues such as poverty, violence, hardship, and hopelessness. She saw one man whose entire day could be brightened by a piece of fruit. A mere piece of fruit.

When you see something as painful and as beautiful as that, everything changes.

My child walked right up and stared directly into the eyes of suffering. She watched in awe as tears of joy collected in a man's eyes simply because of her unexpected presence on a dingy city street on a cold day in December. From that moment on, this child was a full-fledged giver.

When you have the most important things in life—love, faith, and family—there is nothing you own that you can't give away.

Today's Reminder

Today I will make sure my loved ones know they can come to me for truth. If there is something they want to know about the world . . . about life . . . about growing up, I will tell them in words they can understand. Although it is tempting to shelter them from the world's dangers and atrocities, every piece of information and unconditional love is protective armor. Every loving truth makes my loved ones a little stronger, a little more aware, and a little more prepared to navigate the world.

13

Introspection

What if we look for each other today?
The one who's looking for a glimmer of
hope too.
If we look for each other today, we might
just find it.

I THOUGHT OF YOU

Last night, I thought of you,
the one who can barely stand to look in the mirror but
musters the courage to show up anyway.

Last night, I thought of you,
the one unable to sleep because worry pulses through your
veins like caffeine; yet here you are, facing another day.

Last night, I thought of you,
the one living with a choice you're pretty sure was the wrong
one, but you're praying it's not too late to make it right.

Last night, I thought of you,
the one who aches for a loved one's sweet breath but forces
a smile for the ones who are still here breathing.

Last night, I thought of you,
the one who's being pushed away when all you want to do
is help.

Last night, I thought of you,
the one who dreams of what could be, but fear has you paralyzed into inaction.

Last night, I thought of you,
the one whose physical pain seeps into every area of your life; you'd do anything to be set free.

Last night, I thought of you,
the one who wants to live authentically but can already feel the world's rejection if you reveal the real you.

Last night, I thought of you,
the one who wonders: *Is this it? Is this my life?*

I know you cried. I cried with you. It was midnight, and everyone in my house was asleep. I sat in the quiet of my bathroom, and I thought of you. I felt your pain and your questions and your doubt as if they were my own.

I was hoping you'd show up today so I could throw a lifeline into your ocean of despair, so I could breathe oxygen into your tired lungs, so you could take my hand and together we could bridge the gap difficult days often bring.

I thought of you last night; perhaps you thought of me too. Maybe we'll pass each other on the street today, and because we've been thinking of each another, we'll take an extra moment to smile, exchange a look of understanding, or give a knowing glance that could potentially alter the course of the day.

The cause of our pain might be different, but our tears look and feel comfortably familiar—especially at midnight when we're both crying quietly.

What if you look for me today?
The one with different problems but similar pain.
The one who cried last night while you cried last night.
The one who's also looking for a glimmer of hope.
If we look for each other today, we might just find that hope.

Today's Reminder

There is hope in knowing someone understands your suffering. There is hope in hearing someone say, "I see your pain." There is hope in looking out for one another. Isn't this what life is all about? Isn't this what really matters? Reminding the weak they are strong, reminding the brokenhearted they are loved, reminding the lost which way to go. Yes, I think so. Today I will live with eyes and heart wide open.

14

Introspection

I am human, doing the best I can with what I have.
I will put Guilt, Pressure, and Productivity in their place . . . long enough for me to collect myself.

MY INNER FIGHTER

"I don't think I can sink any lower. I don't think I've ever been this far down," I quietly admitted to myself one dark day.

But you created this mess.

You knew better.

You could have prevented this.

Before I throw myself completely under the bus, I stop. I stop right there. I've learned I can come to my own defense. I've learned I don't have to sabotage my chance to get back up when I am down.

I am human, my inner fighter reminds me, tossing out a lifeline. *I'm doing the best I can with what I have. I just don't have much right now—not much energy, strength, patience, or clarity. But it's not going to stay this way forever. I might even feel a little better tomorrow or by Sunday. I'm just going to keep holding on and do the best I can.* Those words put Guilt and Productivity and Pressure and Shame in their place for a while—at least long enough for me to collect myself.

When I find myself in a deep place, down low, I listen to my inner fighter's words of truth. They act as a life preserver when I'm about to go under:

I'm only human, doing the best I can with what I have. I may not have the strength to stand today, but I can hold on. Yes, I can hold on. I might even feel like standing tomorrow or by Sunday. I feel a little more hopeful already.

Today's Reminder

I may not be able to see the end of this challenging season right now, but that doesn't mean it isn't coming. Today I will remember that the hardest part of this struggle will not last forever. I will say, "By this time next week (or next month, or next year), things will be brighter." Until that day comes, I will be kind to myself. I will be patient with myself. I will try to come to my own defense when the bully in my head gets loud. I will remember I'm doing the best I can in the midst of a challenging situation.

15

Encouragement

So take that, One of Those Days! Nobody's throwing in the towel today.

ONE OF THOSE DAYS

It might be One of Those Days
when silences are scarce and meltdowns are abundant;
when pants are too tight, skin is too loose, and the brain is too frazzled;
when failure hangs like fog over the sacred spaces of your home and heart.

It might be One of Those Days. I have them too.
When I do, I look for a little rightness—a little what-is-right-in-my-world.

Notice I say a "little." Because what I am talking about is practically unnoticeable. It's hardly noteworthy. It's definitely not worthy of public sharing—at least not according to societal standards. That's why it's encouraging to me. Looking for what is right in my world, in my day, in my hour is far more encouraging than looking for what is "right" in my world according to mainstream media or popular opinion.

A little right-in-my-world looks like this:
I gave her a back rub when the couch was calling my name.
I gave her a second chance, and she used it for good.
I gave her some help cleaning up that disaster of a room.
She gave me a happy-to-see-you smile when I came to pick her up.

I sacrificed sleep so she didn't have to suffer in the bathroom alone.
I sacrificed my socks because her feet were cold.

I sacrificed a golden opportunity so she could see my face in the audience.
She sacrificed a bit of her ice cream cone without limiting the size of my bite.

I offered to be her excuse if she wanted to leave the party early.
I offered to walk beside her if she needed company.
I offered to stay up and listen awhile.
She offered heartfelt forgiveness when I admitted I messed up.

I encouraged her to try.
I encouraged her to see beyond the surface of herself.
I encouraged her to use her voice, even if it trembled.
She encouraged me to let down my hair and have some fun, and we laughed 'til we cried.

I brushed away the nightmares.
I brushed her hair softly despite our rush to get out the door.
I brushed up on the latest apps so I could be a part of her online world.
She brushed past, but then came back for a hug.

It might be One of Those Days—not enough sun and too much rain,
but it's shining in somebody's world because you are here. You are alive. You exist.
That is what I call "a little rightness."
It's not so little.
In fact, it's a force to be reckoned with.
So take that, One of Those Days! Nobody's throwing in the towel today.

Today's Reminder

Today I will keep track of every kind, helpful, loving, or patient action of mine. I will simply make a hash mark on a sticky note each time I do something positive. At the end of the day, I will look at all those positive actions. There will be more than I expected because I tend to focus on my failings. I must acknowledge the good I do! Just the fact that I am reading this book in order to be more loving toward my people and myself is truly significant! There's my first hash mark! Only Love Today. I will focus on the good.

16

Encouragement

I took that stranger's smile so freely given
to me and I used it as a step stool
to reach my own smile . . . that felt so
far away.

STEP-STOOL SMILE

I reached for my bag of items, and the cashier looked right at me and smiled warmly—
like sunshine warmly;
like Grandma's quilt warmly;
like soothing lullaby warmly.
I looked away.
I didn't want to be seen. I felt ugly. Unkempt. A mess of sorts.
But there he was, smiling at me. Looking right at me like I wasn't ugly. Like I wasn't a mess.

For one brief moment, I realized the ugliness I felt inside might not be apparent on the outside.
For one brief moment, I realized maybe I was being too hard on myself (again).
For one brief moment, I realized I didn't have to hide.
I took that stranger's smile, so freely given to me, and I used it as a step stool
to reach my own smile, my own courage, my own love
that felt so far away.
Now here I am.
Some days, I am the smiler.
Some days, I am the one who wants to look away.
When I am the smiler, I smile warmly. A warm smile has the power to go down deep and shoo away the ugly thoughts that make a good person want to hide.
When I am the one who wants to look away, I don't.
I take that warmth so freely given to me, and I hold it to my face like sunshine,
like my grandma's quilt,
like a soothing lullaby
bringing love to the hurting places in my soul I cannot reach today.

Today's Reminder

Today when I encounter another human being, I will smile warmly; I never know what darkness my smile might lift. If I am on the receiving end of a warm smile, I will use it to reach the hurting places I've been unable to reach. Whether I am the giver or a receiver today, this smile will be a beautiful sight to behold. I'm going to bring the love, embrace the love, and be the love.

17

Hope

Moving on can be difficult and painful,
but there's something to be said for
becoming a better version of yourself
in the process.

When You Find Yourself in Unfamiliar Territory

Over the summer, we moved to a new state. My younger daughter repeatedly says, "I still don't feel like this is home. It feels like we're on a trip and we need to get back."

Sometimes she says it through tears. Other times she says it matter-of-factly. Sometimes she even laughs about it. This fluctuation of emotions pretty much summarizes the ups and downs that accompany moving. I want to make her love this new place, but I don't have the power to do that. I *do* have the power to make her feel a little less lost, though. And I think these actions could help anyone who's feeling uprooted, a little lost, or in unfamiliar territory.

You call an old friend to hear her voice. When it sounds the same, you feel comforted. You realize there are just some things time and distance cannot touch.

You find a place to walk and think. Make it a small loop so it becomes familiar quickly. Then you feel like you've been here before. We all want to feel like we've been here before.

You venture to new places and meet new people, but you

remember to be patient with yourself if you make a wrong turn or forget someone's name. You celebrate the fact that you had the courage to put yourself out there.

You recognize the growth that's occurring within you as a result of this challenge. Moving on, literally or figuratively, can be difficult and painful, but there's something to be said for becoming a better version of yourself in the process.

You listen to your favorite songs on repeat. You know the words. Like certain beloved faces, there are just some lyrics you know by heart.

Finally, and most importantly, you get a soft pillowcase that feels like a comfy old T-shirt, and you establish a new ritual. That's what my daughter did. Every night, without fail, she says, "Put your head on my pillow, Mama. Feel how soft and cozy it is?" It seemed odd at first. She never did that in the old house, but now it's our bedtime ritual. And for just a split second, with her breath on my face, it feels an awful lot like home to me too.

Today's Reminder

As I go through my day, I will pay close attention to the sights, sounds, and feelings that bring comfort to me; perhaps I will find a little piece of home in a song, a face, a fragrance, or a favorite food. And for a brief moment, perhaps I'll feel like I am exactly where I belong.

18

Hope

Today might just be the day your life's
message intersects
with a heart longing for what only you
can deliver.

LIFE ON REPEAT

Teacher, do you tire of circle time? Do you feel like you review the same rules over and over and over? Do you sound out the same words, show the same spelling patterns, and answer the same questions year after year? I imagine you do.

Nurse, do you tire of taking vitals and bodily fluids? Do you see the same health issues day in and day out? Do you feel like you walk the same halls, administer the same doses, and whisper the same assurances? I suspect you do.

Mail carrier, do you tire of damaged packages and insufficient postage? Do you ever long to open a new mailbox? Do you wish you could personally deliver handwritten notes to actual people and see their joy? I have a sneaking suspicion you do.

Cashier, do you tire of slow conveyor belts, unorganized coupons, and unsmiling customers? Do your feet ache from standing in the same place for hours every day? Do you hear the same bubblegum battle between parents and children day in and day out? I'm pretty sure you do.

Parent, do you tire of grumpy small people, missing shoes, and that dreaded question, *What's for dinner?* Do you wipe the same noses, pick up the same wet towels, defuse the same sibling squabbles day in and day out? I know you do.

Musician, do you tire of bad song requests, callused fingers, and lack of appreciation? Do you long for a new crowd, a new venue, a new stool to prop your foot on? Do you get sick of wondering if this dream is going anywhere? I suppose you do.

But here's the thing: you just never know when you'll be in the middle of that redundant message, task, or duty, and suddenly something will happen to let you know this time is different.

That song you've longed to write appears before you.

That patient turns the corner.

That kindergartener begins to read.

That woman weeps when you hand her a long-awaited letter from a military base.

That customer needs that unexpected smile.

That grown child says, "Thanks, Mom and Dad. You are the reason I made it through."

Suddenly your life on repeat is someone's divine sign, someone's lifesaver, someone's second chance, someone's voice of an angel, someone's silver lining, someone's hope not lost.

As you know, you cannot predict when that day will come. It could be a slow Monday morning. It could be a rainy Friday afternoon when the traffic is really bad. It could be the day that follows a rough night. It could be when you are about to throw in the towel. Yes, it could be that day.

So I beg you to carry on.

Burp that baby for the nine hundredth time.

Shine those windows like a boss.

Lift your voice from the back row of the choir for the whole wide world to hear.

Write beautiful words until you can write no more.

These are the redundant actions of an everyday hero.

Today just might be the day your life's message intersects with a heart longing for what only you can deliver.

So please, I beg you, carry on.

Today's Reminder

Sometimes I need to be reminded I am human and that my feelings, woes, and frustrations are valid. Sometimes I need to be reminded that my daily efforts make a difference. Sometimes I need to be reminded that there will be rewards in the toil, and when that day comes, I will be grateful I chose to carry on.

19

Encouragement

When you invest in what matters most,
it pays off in the deepest chambers of a
grateful heart.

A Return on Your Investment

There's a woman stumbling down a dark hallway. She's getting up, not for herself but for those who count on her. "I am here," she whispers into the darkness as she helps her precious ones face another day.

I see a return on her investment.

There's a man, up before the sun, packing a lunch and writing a note to his child that will be tucked inside. "You make me smile," he writes today.

I see a return on his investment.

There's a man keeping a bedside vigil in a quiet hospital room. He wants his beloved to see a familiar face when she wakes. "I won't leave you," he pledges.

I see a return on his investment.

There's a young lady rehearsing what she'll say to protect a friend who is unable to defend herself. "You can count on me," she vows.

I see a return on her investment.

There's a bus driver opening the doors and smiling through the pain. "I'm so happy to see you," he says to his precious cargo as they noisily board.

I see a return on his investment.

There's a woman gearing up for a difficult conversation, a life-saving one. "I won't let you go through it alone," she will say before her loved one is completely lost.

I see a return on her investment.

I do.

Investments of time, presence, courage, and heart
are of the most priceless kind.
The payoff is often hard to see,
and doesn't always come quickly enough,
especially when your burdens are heavy and your eyes are weary;
but I see it—that return on your priceless investment.
I see that silent "Thank you" in her eyes.
I see the way he reaches for your hand without a second thought.
I see the way she breathes easier when you are near.
I see the way you bring comfort in a way no one else can.
You might not see it,
especially if your burdens are heavy and your eyes are weary;
but that investment you are making,
and those words you are saying,
they are paying off.
They are paying off
in ways you cannot even begin to imagine,
but I hope you will try.
When you invest in what matters most,
it pays off
in the deepest chambers of a grateful heart.

Today's Reminder

Today I will remind myself of these three truths: (1) the most important investments I can make each day are relational investments; (2) the most important actions of my day are not on the to-do list; and (3) the most important thing to my loved ones is me—my presence, my attention, my love. Pausing amid the duties and challenges of everyday life to love and be loved is not easy, but it is essential and the rewards are great.

20

Hope

There is strength in knowing today *is another word for* second chance.

YOU'VE GOT TODAY

If yesterday nearly brought you to your knees,
if recent events have left you broken,
if you can't bear to see that look of disappointment one more time,
if hope is a stranger,
if you can't remember ever feeling this tired,
if you can't quite seem to catch a break,
read on . . .
You've got something on your side,
and it's easy to forget you have this
when you're coming off a long night, a long month, or a long year.
You've got today.

You, with the achy bones as you crawl into your child's bed
for story time;
you, with the tireless hands whose love never runs out;
you, who are never at a loss for words when it comes to
defending your precious ones;
you, whose babies will never be too heavy to carry;
you've got today.
You've got a second wind.
You've got a new dawn.
You've got another chance.
You've got an opportunity you didn't have before.
It's called *today.*
It's easy to forget you have this
when you're coming off a long night, a long month, or a
long year.
So when you are ready, gather your strength and lift your
voice up to say:
yesterday may have left me breathless,
yesterday may have reduced my options,
yesterday may have hit me where it hurts,
but that was yesterday.
I am still here.
I am still here.
There is strength in knowing yesterday is gone.
There is strength in knowing *today* is another word for
second chance.

Today's Reminder

If I got out of bed today, that is hope. If I shed some cleansing tears or thought about my options, that is hope. If I have considered ways to stop self-destructive behavior, that is hope. If I have taken one small step forward, that is hope. If I have garnered the strength to love someone today, that is hope. Right now I will place my hand in front of my lips and feel the air expel. I am still breathing. I'm still fighting. The moment I got up to face the world was the moment I decided not to give up. That is hope.

21

Introspection

Breathing room.
I've heard it does wonders for a withering soul trying to find its way back to life.

Breathing Room

For just one day
I need an unmade bed no one critiques.
I need a body no one evaluates.
I need a mistake void of exasperation.

For just one day
I need a project no one supervises or crowds around.
I need a breath no one stifles.
I need a set of teeth no one examines before I head out the door.

For just one day
I need an idea no one contaminates.
I need an opinion that might be unpopular among high achievers.
I need a pace that goes along with the song in my head.

For just one day
I need a morning ungoverned,
a performance unassessed,
a meal eaten with my fingers,
a hairstyle that's all me.

Would it be so bad to let me have it? An hour, a day, a season of my own?
If you ease up, would it really be the end of the world?
I don't think so.
I think it might be the opposite.
I think it would be the start of my world opening up,
the introduction of new possibilities,
added space where my feet could move and my colors could shine.
I think it would be a place where my forgotten joy could bubble up to the surface
as my confidence finds wings.

Just for one day
could I get a little breathing room?
I've heard it does wonders for a withering soul trying to find its way back to life.

Today's Reminder

I think I could use a little breathing room today. I think my beloved people could too. So today I'll lower the bar. I'll give it a rest. I'll overlook the weeds and see the flowers in my life instead. It won't be the end of the world if I do. It could be the start of something quite hopeful and enduring.

22

Encouragement

Loving responses can mean the difference between light and total darkness.

LIGHTER LONGER

It's staying lighter longer. We've got more daylight, I think to myself as I take a walk at dusk.

I open the door, and home hits all my senses with its inhabitants, its duties, and its disarray. I brace myself for what might come. (You just never know.)

But it can be lighter longer at home, too, I am reminded as I close the door. Golden sunbeams manage to find their way in.

When morning comes too soon,
when clothes don't feel right,
when schoolwork brings tears,
when emotions flare,
when friendships hurt,
when opinions collide,
I could tell her to straighten up.
I could tell her to stop crying this instant.
I could tell her that is not a real problem.
I could tell her I can't deal right now.
I could. I could say those things and cut off the light,
or I could make it lighter longer:
"You must feel pretty sad right now."
"This math concept can be so tricky. Let's take a look."

"You'll get through this. I have faith in you."
"Would an extra five minutes help?"
"What seems to be the trouble? I'm listening."
These responses don't come easily, especially in moments of friction,
but they can mean the difference between
connection and separation,
hope and despair,
giving up and prevailing.
These loving responses can mean the difference between light and total darkness.
The walls of our home aren't always an easy place to be,
but if we let in more light
through loving words and actions,
it can be a better day, and possibly a better life, for us all.

Today's Reminder

Today when a loved one is struggling or we are in conflict with each another, I will ask, "How can I help?" This question brings down defenses, validates feelings, and puts us on the same team. A helpful and healing light is produced when we know someone is for us, not against us, and seeking to support us in ways that allow us to feel heard.

23

Introspection

When I begin to go down the path of worry,
I stop myself by saying one word: trust.

REPLACE WORRY WITH TRUST

I spent much of my child's early years worrying. Would she ever be ready to take those training wheels off her bike? Would she ever learn to swim without protest? Would she ever learn to read like her classmates? In my state of worry, I lost precious moments—moments to enjoy my child "as is."

When she turned six and began reading, riding, and swimming, I had an epiphany. Much of what I worried about had a way of working out in time—in my child's own time. By living in a state of worry, I was robbing myself of the gifts of today.

With clarity I realized these painful truths about living with worry:

Worry can remove you from the most beautiful moments of your life, as if you aren't even there.

Worry can steal meaningful experiences right from your memory bank, as if they didn't even happen.

Worry can prevent you from experiencing happiness, passion, and joy, as if you merely existed rather than truly lived.

Now things are different.

When I begin to go down the path of worry, I stop myself by saying one word: *trust.*

Trust that worrying will do nothing to change the outcome.

Trust that my child will be where she needs to be in her own time.

Trust that things will work out as they should.

When I choose to focus on all that is going *right* in my life and let go of what I can't control, I am free to live more and love more in the precious day at hand.

Today's Reminder

What if I stopped worrying about things I can't control and started focusing on things I can *control? What would it do for my attitude? My sleep? My health? My outlook? How would it positively impact the ones with whom I share my life? Perhaps it would lessen their worries if I surrendered mine with the word* trust. *Today I vow to free myself from fruitless worry and focus solely on the things I can change.*

24

Introspection

Don't stay in a place where you cannot thrive.
Come back. Come back.
Love can bring you home.

COME BACK

It doesn't take long to cross over those fragile state lines.
From a state of calm
to a state of impatience.

From a state of caring
to a state of apathy.

From a state of presence
to a state of distraction.

From a state of hope
to a state of despair.

From a state of joy
to a state of infuriation.

Just one lost homework sheet,
just one mediocre work review,
just one blow to your self-esteem,
just one wrong turn,
just one stupid mistake,
just one more snow day,
just one more rejection,
just one more letdown.
Before you know it, you've crossed over
to find yourself in that place you never wanted to be (again).

Don't stay there.
Don't go any further down the road to the state of regret.
This trip called life is too short and too precious to spend in
such dismal places.
Come back. Come back.

Forgive yourself.
Forgive the one who wronged you.

Say you're sorry.
Say you're not finished yet; you've only just begun.

Turn up a good song.
Call up a good friend.

Hug the person nearest you.
Hug the person furthest out of reach.

Put riches in an empty cup.
Fill your cup.

Walk outside and spot something beautiful.
Dig inside and discover something beautiful you thought
was gone.

Come back. Come back.
Crossing those fragile state lines is part of being human.

Don't stay in a place where you cannot thrive.
Come back. Come back. No map necessary.
Love can bring you home.

Today's Reminder

In moments of frustration, challenge, and overwhelm, I vow to look directly into the faces of my loved ones before I respond. In that critical pause, I will see people who count on me to care for them, love them, and guide them. I will see people who are learning how to live by watching me live. Taking that moment to look at them, really look at them, will enable me to come back to a place where my voice can be heard instead of hurtful.

25

Hope

In the act of envisioning the person you
hope to be,
it becomes a real possibility
instead of a far-fetched dream.

NOT BEYOND REPAIR

It might be hard to imagine the *after* version of yourself
when you are standing on the *before* side.
Too many flaws,
too many failings,
too many shortcomings,
too many mistakes
to think you could ever be what you hope to be.
But the fact that you're standing there,
taking that difficult look inward to see what needs repairing,
well, that's something.
We know change doesn't happen overnight,
at least not the lasting kind,
so please consider this:
as you stand there envisioning how you might look if
you were
a little more calm,
a little more positive,
a little more grateful,
a little more content,
a little more present,
you've just gotten one step closer to the *after* version of
yourself
and one step further away from the *before.*
In the act of envisioning the person you hope to be,
it becomes a real possibility
instead of a far-fetched dream—
one you couldn't have seen
if you hadn't taken that courageous step away
from *before.*

Today's Reminder

I would like to become more __________. I am going to picture someone who embodies this characteristic. During the most important connection times with my loved ones, I will emulate this person. At departure times, reuniting times, mealtimes, and bedtimes, I will try to consistently display the character trait of __________, as this person does. By acting like the person I want to become, I get closer to who I aspire to be.

26

Introspection

On the other side of letdown is belief—
belief that your story is far from over.

ON THE OTHER SIDE

The times my child cried as a baby all blur together in my mind. But the times she cries now, those stand out as I witness her pain, desperately wanting to spare her from it.

But I can't.

And I shouldn't.

That is not my role.

As my daughter sat silently in the backseat after a recent painful experience, I grappled with what to say. This is what came out:

"Although this really hurts, you are gaining a valuable experience that will help you get through the next challenge you face. When something feels familiar, even something painful or disappointing, it helps you overcome the next obstacle."

I gave her a few examples that personified uncomfortable

feelings and how past experience helps us deal with them. It sounded like this:

Hey, Disappointment, I know you. And I know you eventually pass.

Hey, Frustration, I've dealt with you before. You didn't stop me then, and you won't stop me now.

Hey, Obstacle, you tried to stop me, but I made it to the other side. That's what I am going to do today.

I told my daughter that facing pain and disappointment can be like walking into a familiar place. They don't feel quite as scary if you've been there before.

A few days later, I noticed the sadness in her eyes had been replaced with a fiery spark. I recognized determination, courage, and strength. She had a plan, she said. She wasn't going to let this setback keep her down, she said. As I watched her walk into the building where her heart had been shattered a few days prior, I realized,

> *On the other side of disappointment is desire—desire to create a different outcome next time.*
>
> *On the other side of letdown is belief—belief that your story is far from over.*
>
> *On the other side of pain is strength—strength you didn't know you had until you had to dig deep to find it.*
>
> *On the other side of hurt is gratitude—gratitude for those who love you and stand by you in your pain.*
>
> *On the other side of despair is connection—connection that comes from recognizing a familiar look of pain in someone else's eyes and reaching out your hand.*

Shielding my child from struggle, challenge, pain, and disappointment is tempting. But the characteristics I most want her to develop are often born from a place of adversity. So that one day, when she comes face-to-face with sadness, trauma, loss, or hopelessness, she will not be paralyzed with fear or give up because it's too hard. Instead she will say, "I know you. I've seen you before. You cannot take me down. In fact, I'll face you and come out stronger than I was before."

Today's Reminder

Perhaps when my child tells me she wants to try something new, I need to offer support. Perhaps when he tells me he's hurt, I need to recognize his pain. Perhaps when she's telling me she's got it covered, I need to step back. By listening to what they're telling me they need, I'll confirm the power of their inner voices—the voices that know what they need to thrive. Although it might feel scary or painful to not rush in and fix or help, it will result in independence, growth, and newfound confidence. My beloveds are learning to fly. Let me respect their internal navigation systems and watch them soar.

27

Hope

When you find yourself enveloped in the shadows, I hope someone shines a light.

THAT IS MY HOPE

When you find yourself at the end of your rope, I hope
someone pulls you back.
When you feel alone, I hope someone sits beside you.
When you find yourself enveloped in the shadows, I hope
someone shines a light.

That is my hope.

When you are uncertain, I hope someone gives you assurance.
When you are judged, I hope someone defends you.
When you find yourself feeling different from the rest, I hope someone spots a common thread that binds you together.
That is my hope.

When you don't have the words, I hope someone speaks for you.
When you are lost, I hope someone leads you home.
When you bleed, I hope someone applies pressure.
That is my hope.

When you bravely sing out, I hope someone's voice joins in.
When you wonder if you matter, I hope someone reminds you that you do.
When you cry out in question, I hope someone answers.
That is my hope.

Today's Reminder

I know from personal experience that people who are smiling on the outside can very well be hurting on the inside. Those people are the ones who perhaps feel most alone because their pain is hidden well. Today I will think about those in my life who might be hurting. If I don't extend love or kindness to them today, perhaps they won't receive any. But if I do—if I do—perhaps the timing will be perfect, and they will say, "How did you know? This was just what I needed." My hope and my prayer is that I will help others feel less alone today.

28

ENCOURAGEMENT

Sometimes we just need a moment—and every moment is a chance to start anew.

LOVE'S NAVIGATION

"Did you cry when you were looking for him?" Avery asked the morning after our cat Banjo had gone missing.

"No. Why?" I asked, curious.

"I could hear you calling and calling for him outside my bedroom window when I was trying to go to sleep."

I swallowed the lump in my throat. "Were *you* crying?" I asked her.

"No," she said. "Because we have a family code, you know."

I did not know.

"It's *No Family Member Left Behind*," she explained.

"Did you come up with that yourself?" I asked, stunned.

"Yes. In our family, we'd never leave without each other. You'd never leave without me."

All at once, the suffocating weight of "not enough" lifted from my weary chest. Yesterday had not been a stellar day. I was not myself. I could count my mistakes and believe me, I did. But here she was, my little messenger of grace, reminding me of a healing truth God knew I desperately needed:

even on days when I can't tear myself away from my distractions . . .

even on days when I overreact to something trivial . . .

even on days when I obsess over bulges and wrinkles and things that don't matter one bit in the end . . .

even on days when I want to lock myself in the bathroom and weep . . .

even on days when I am at my worst . . .

I am still the person in my loved ones' world who would do anything to spare them from pain and harm. I am still the person who would not leave them, no matter the cost.

Perhaps you know someone who would make the same sacrifice; I bet you do.

So when you see that less-than-perfect person staring back at you in the mirror, I ask you to extend grace rather than judgment.

You are not the sum of your distractions.

You are not composed of your flaws and failings.

You are someone's home base, even when you get a little off course.

But love can bring you back.

Love's navigation never fails.

Today's Reminder

I don't have to be a superhero today. I don't have to save the world. I'll just hold someone I love tightly in my arms and be home base. I don't have to predict the future. I don't have to see a silver lining in the latest catastrophe. I'll just notice the sky above my head and be home base. I don't have to know all the words. I don't have to speak with conviction. I'll just say, "I am here," and be home base.

29

Hope

It's a wondrous thing to go through life seeing space for possibilities instead of limited options.

MAKING SPACE FOR POSSIBILITIES

Lately, when I open a cabinet or a drawer, I don't have to brace myself. In fact, a feeling of peace overcomes me because I look in and see that everything is in order. My daughter Natalie had asked me what she could do to earn some money. I mentioned the exploding drawers and cabinets, and she's been tackling them, one by one.

This is the same girl who once had exploding folders, backpacks, and messy piles of disarray.

Her very special fourth grade teacher noticed how much my child was struggling to organize her many academic assignments and loose papers. She told Natalie, "When I was young, I was just like you. I had so many neat things going on in my brain, it was hard to keep up with the papers."

As a team, Natalie and her beloved teacher created a color-coded binder system to help my daughter stay organized. She still uses this particular tool as a successful middle school student.

I remember the first night Natalie came home with her color-coded binder. She had the right papers in the right folders, and she knew exactly what she needed to do that night for homework.

"Mrs. Reynolds was just like me when she was my age," she said proudly. "So many good ideas in her head. She told me how I could become a great organizer. Look. Look at how organized I am."

I nearly cried. I'd always worried about the pitfalls of my daughter's disorganization but was convinced that was just the way it was going to be. Natalie sitting before me with all her ducks in a row was a sight I never expected to see. Although it was just the beginning of her new trait, I knew the impact of her teacher's belief was going to be profound.

Little did I know how it would impact my own life.

With new eyes, I began looking at my loved ones' areas of "weakness" differently. I stopped assuming their weaknesses would never be strengths. It didn't take long to see what I'd done to myself over the years with regard to my shaky math skills, my technology ineptitude, and my fear of public speaking. *Maybe with the proper tools and a little belief, I could overcome, too*, I thought for the first time. *Maybe I could actually be something I wrote off a long time ago.*

And I have. So have the people I love. It's a wondrous thing to go through life seeing space for possibilities instead of limited options.

I invite you to join me in seeing what isn't yet but could be.
Might we be the ones who see potential where others see a problem.
Might we be the ones who provide a helpful tool where others offer resistance.
Might we be the ones who lift up where others write off.
Might we be the ones who say, "It's possible."
With the right tools and a little belief, we could change someone's inner dialogue and future outlook to make space for dreams unimagined.
What a wondrous thing it would be.

Today's Reminder

Today I will look at perceived weaknesses in my loved ones and myself with new eyes. I will ask myself how a weakness might be a hidden strength. I will ask to see what isn't yet, but could be *with a little time and guidance. By believing change can happen, the sky of possibilities opens up, and hope swells.*

30

ENCOURAGEMENT

The positive ripples created by showing up for those we love are endless and everlasting.

THE ART OF SHOWING UP

We arrived at the hospital as the sun was setting. Although a good portion of visiting hours remained, there was an urgency in my husband's stride. Perhaps he instinctively knew something I didn't.

Unfortunately, nothing could have prepared Scott for what he was about to see.

His grandpa was hooked to ominous-looking machines that beeped and hushed at a slow, rhythmic pace. There were countless tubes attached to his body. Like a clump of rubber bands, it was difficult to figure out where one tube ended and the other began.

"He is in a deep sleep right now, son," the nurse informed him. "You may want to come back tomorrow."

As if he didn't hear her, my husband pulled up a chair next to his grandfather's bedside and sat down. He gently wrapped his strong, slender fingers around his grandpa's translucent hands, lined with protruding veins.

"Do you remember the double header in Anderson, Grandpa?" His casual tone suggested the two of them were sitting side by side on a porch swing or relaxing on the back patio.

"I smashed a line drive to right field only to get thrown out at first base." He laughed out loud. "Speed was never my forte, was it Grandpa?"

My husband turned to me, as if suddenly remembering I was

there. I was standing off in the corner, partially not to intrude on this sacred moment, and partially to hide my tear-stained face.

"My grandpa never told me when he was going to come to one of my college baseball games," he explained, as one would bring others up to speed if they missed the first part of a conversation.

He continued wistfully. "It didn't matter if it was a weak team and required a four-hour drive to get there. I'd look up in the stands, and there he'd be."

My husband appeared to be smiling at me, but I think he was actually smiling to himself. He added quietly, "Papaw would just show up."

He then turned back to his most loyal fan, cradling his grandpa's pliable hand lovingly within his own. "Thank you for showing up, Papaw."

Scott's grandfather died peacefully not long after our visit. At his memorial service, many people spoke of his incredible lifetime achievements as a star athlete, successful coach, and school superintendent.

Now, decades later, I think one of this man's greatest contributions was his influence on my husband's life.

I see it when my daughter says, "Dad showed up at school for lunch today, and I didn't even know he was coming!"

I see it when my husband says, "My sister and brother are running in a race this weekend. If we get on the road early tomorrow, we can show up and surprise them."

I see it when there's a community service day in our city, and he says, "Maybe they could use some extra hands."

The art of showing up.

Some people do it so well—they're willing to forgo their own agendas and their own timetables because they understand the vital importance of presence.

The art of showing up.

A simple act that becomes a representation of who you are and a beautiful legacy you one day leave behind.

We all have the opportunity to be that person who "shows up" today.

Today's Reminder

Today I will acknowledge the vital importance of being one who shows up and act on it. I will not let my own issues, busy schedule, or lack of knowing what to say interfere with giving a gift people will remember their whole lives. Today I will write the words Just show up *in my calendar next to someone's name. My presence and support—whether in person, written in a card, or spoken during a phone call—matters to someone. It also matters to me. The positive ripples created by showing up for those I love are endless and everlasting.*

31

Introspection

The next time you feel like you're drifting away,
remember you've anchored yourself in love.

ANCHORED IN LOVE

He said he just can't seem to get it together,
but he was holding his child's hand.
He had the most important things together.

She said she lost it,
but she'd managed to find her voice to offer remorse.
She lost it briefly but didn't let it go forever.

He said he failed him,
but in the same breath he was asking how he could
reach him.
He might've failed, but he hadn't given up.

She said her life is one mad dash,
but she'd gathered her child in her arms and held on for a
while.
She stopped for what mattered.

He said he doesn't feel like he's doing any good,
but he knows which princess pajamas are her favorite and
plants a sturdy kiss on her cheek when they part ways.
That is good. That is good.

The next time you find yourself falling apart, losing it,
doubting, wishing, and wondering, remember this:
On that cheek you kissed,
in that hand you held,
in that apology you offered,
in that reliable embrace you gave
is proof that you're doing better than you think.

You encourage when you feel discouraged.
You love when you feel unlovable.
You heal when you're broken.
You save when you're going under.
You reach when you're barely holding on.

The next time you feel like you're drifting away,
remember you've anchored yourself with love.
Let that keep you afloat today.

Today's Reminder

In the ups and downs of life, it's hard to grasp what really matters, but I am trying. Today is a good day to acknowledge my efforts and what those efforts mean to those who count on me. I will embrace today for what it is: a brand-new chance to love and be loved. Even the briefest moment of loving connection holds the power to evoke healing and hope for the giver and the receiver. Today is a new day. I pledge to let love lead my words and actions.

32

Encouragement

Your lowest point might just be your finest hour.

COMEBACK STORY

Note to Self:
The lonely self,
the broken-hearted self,
the hopeless self,
the worrier self,
the hanging-by-a-thread self,
the not-myself-today self,
the looking-for-a-bright-spot self,
this one's for you:

You got back up when you could've broken down.
You kept shining when you could've faded to gray.
You held on when you could've let go.
You kept your head above water when you could've gone under.

You kept coming back when you could've said, "I have nothing left to give."
You realize what this makes you, right?
A living, breathing Comeback Story.
You come back to love even when you can barely manage a smile.
You come back to love when you are completely overwhelmed by life.
You come back to love when you have no clue what you're doing.
You come back to love when you're hungry and tired.
You come back to love when you feel worthless and inadequate.
You come back to love when it's the last thing you want to do.
You come back to love when you feel as though you have no love to give.
You're a living, breathing Comeback Story.
Let that change your view on this less-than-stellar morning.
Let that change your view on the disarray that surrounds you.
Let that change your view of the puffy eyes and saggy skin you see in the mirror.
Let that change your view on the mistakes of yesterday replaying in your head.
Your lowest point might just be your finest hour.
Because you came back.
You keep coming back.
For love.
For love.
Let that sink in for a moment.
You're a living, breathing Comeback Story.
Let that be your victory song today.

Today's Reminder

I am stuck today. It doesn't mean I will be stuck forever. It doesn't mean I have to quickly get unstuck (although that is typically my first response). I will tell myself something kind: "It's okay to be stuck today." Then I'll tell myself something brave: "But stick around; something good is around the bend." And then I'll wait. Because comebacks aren't found on a timeline—they're found within.

33

Hope

I've discovered that to deny my story hurts more than the story itself, so I've chosen to own it.

OWNING YOUR STORY

You never wanted to know how to survive divorce.
You never wanted to know the joys and heartaches of autism.
You never wanted to know the signs of addiction.
But you do.

You never wanted to know rock bottom.
You never wanted to know how to leave an abusive relationship.
You never wanted to know it was possible to bounce back after a financial crisis.
But you do.

You never wanted to know the pain of caring for a parent who doesn't remember you.
You never wanted to be the strong one.
You never wanted to know the car could be a safe place to cry.
But you do.

You never wanted to know a family could break.
You never wanted to know how to put the pieces back together in a new way.
You never wanted to know a new normal.
But you do.

You never wanted to know the perfect response when someone stares at your child.
You never wanted to know the courage it takes to ask for help.
You never wanted to know how to find joy after having lost it for so long.
But you do.

You never wanted to know it's sometimes necessary to sever ties in order to have inner peace.
You never wanted to know how hard it is to say to yourself, "Change begins today. My loved ones deserve better."
You never wanted to know the weight that's lifted when you say to yourself, "It wasn't my fault."
But you do. You do.

Perhaps as time has passed, you've discovered that to deny your story hurts more than the story itself, so you've chosen to own it.

To speak out, even when your voice shakes.
To tell the truth, even when it's not pretty.
To encourage someone else, even when you can barely encourage yourself.
To get up and face the world, even when you can barely look in the mirror.

The tears that streak your face at the most inopportune times of the day, at the most inappropriate moments, are the lines of your story. Each time you own them, someone else is not alone in his or her story. Your jumbled mess, whether whispered as a prayer to one or shouted in desperation to thousands, could be the message someone needs right now. And perhaps by sharing, your pain will ease, your hope will grow, your tomorrow will look a little bit brighter.

Today's Reminder

I never wanted to know ____________________________, but I do. This experience has impacted my life in negative ways, but it has also shaped my life in beneficial ways. Today I will celebrate the silver linings on the edges of my mess. I will think about how I can use what I've learned to help someone else carry on despite the struggle. Helping someone else through my story will accentuate the silver linings of my mess, my story, and my life. Blessed to be the messenger, I will shine on.

34

Hope

Uncertainty loses its power
in the presence of love.

THE CERTAINTY OF LOVE

Today you might not get any closer to resolving your current issue. You may not get the relief that comes with knowing why or the peace that comes with gaining clarity. You may get deafening silence when you look into faces that are supposed to have all the answers, and that will be hard.

Uncertainty is shaky ground. Uncertainty is not a comfortable place to be. Uncertainty causes worry, doubt, anger, hopelessness. And those emotions only strengthen uncertainty's grip and make the place you are in feel even shakier.

Here's what I do when uncertainty keeps me from sleeping, thinking positively, and being at peace: I ground myself in love.

I listen to the steady breathing in the bed next to me at 10:55 p.m.

I creep into her bedroom at 6:22 a.m. so I can watch her sleep for a few minutes before I wake her.

I watch the door of the bus at 4:36 p.m. so I can see my middle schooler smile at me.

I call my mom at 8:42 a.m., hearing her warm hello before she even picks up.

In a period of uncertainty in my life, I find great comfort in the certainty of my love for my people and in their love for me. When the ground is shaky, I find great comfort in the consistency of these loving rituals.

If you haven't yet discovered this hope-filled truth, let me share it with you:

Uncertainty loses its power in the presence of love.

It's worth repeating and absorbing.

Uncertainty loses its power in the presence of love.

If today finds your world crumbling down around you, if there are more questions than answers, if things are not what they should be, try this:

Try watching your loved ones depart. They might even turn back to wave.

Try watching them during a practice or performance. They might even look up and smile to see if you are watching.

Try watching her eat her favorite cereal. See how that milk drips down that beautiful face.

Try watching him find you in a crowd. Watch how his chest relaxes when you make eye contact.

Try watching them sleep. Look at the peace settled on their faces.

Although very few things are predictable in this life, there might just be one thing that remains constant: love for the face that belongs to you.

What you planned or expected might be shaken up, and your world might be crumbling down, but you, my friend, are grounded in love.

Today's Reminder

I am searching for answers right now, as are many people. Someone is wondering if it's time to date after being alone for many years. Someone is wondering when her unfamiliar surroundings will feel familiar. Someone is wondering how she'll get through her first holiday without her loved one. Someone is waiting on test results. There might be more questions than answers for many of us right now, but there is certainty in beloved faces and warm blankets. In the face of uncertainty, I will open my arms and let love propel me forward.

35

Introspection

Transformation does not happen at the end
of the trial; it happens in the midst of it.

IN THE BECOMING

Perhaps it's been awhile since you saw the sun.
Perhaps it's been awhile since you laughed until tears ran down your face.
Perhaps it's been awhile since you believed things are going to be okay.
But in these murky waters you continue to forge on.
In this pitch-black darkness, you continue to feel your way.
In this hanging-by-a-thread-moment, you continue to hang in there.
Maybe you haven't noticed.
Perhaps all you see is the toll this trial is taking on your appearance, your family, your spirit. Perhaps you only feel yourself becoming more pessimistic, more hopeless, and more impatient with each passing day.
It's hard to see what you are becoming when you are focused on holding on.
Let me shed a little light on the subject:
Your presence is proof this trial will not defeat you. Each day that you show up, you are becoming more.
More resilient.
More experienced.
More enlightened.
More intuitive.
More faithful.
More informed.
More sympathetic.
More enduring.

Transformation does not happen at the end of the trial; it happens in the midst of it. Right now. In the becoming.

So please make note. Please consider the proof. Please acknowledge the significance of your presence today.

Even though it may not look or feel like it right now, you are in the process of becoming an improved version of yourself.

There is great significance in the *becoming* part of your trial. And today, here you are, mastering it quite beautifully.

Today's Reminder

I am tired of the pain. I am tired of the waiting. I am tired of the unknown. But I know more about myself than I did before this trial began. I have more compassion for the enduring pain of others. I am more appreciative of the everyday moments of connection with my family and friends. I have withstood more than I ever thought I could. I haven't seen the sun in awhile, but I know it's there because my growth beneath its nourishing light cannot be denied.

36

Encouragement

Today has hope yesterday doesn't have.

REMEMBER WHAT DAY IT IS

Lately my younger daughter has been curious about what she was like as a toddler. In my sock drawer, I keep my favorite picture of her when she was three. She'd carefully donned an oversized necklace with a fake blue "diamond" before we left the house. I'd waited patiently for once. In return, I received a smile so big it scrunched up her eyes with joy.

"Tell me about me," Avery's nine-year-old self says now.

I look at that picture and think.

My child knows letdown. She knows distance, agitation, and impatience. She knows what it feels like to have her hopes crushed like a paper airplane. She knows worry that makes it impossible to sleep. She knows confusion and the sound of my sobs. She knows a mama who breaks dishes in frustration. She knows a mama who chose to hold inanimate objects instead of her child's hand far too many times. She knows when it's time to plug her ears and shut her eyes. She knows things I wish I could take back.

Looking at that picture left me wondering if I've let my baby down one too many times, if the scars run too deep, if the hurts are too great. *I could've done better*, I think to myself more often than I'd like to admit.

But then I remember what day it is.

It is today. It is not yesterday.

Today all hope is not lost. Oh no—hope is not lost.

Today I can follow through.

Today I can listen, really listen.

Today I can say, "You can count on me," and mean it with every fiber of my being.

Today I can use *soul-building words* and swallow hurtful ones.

Today I can see what is good before I see what needs improvement.

Today I can pick my battles and choose love every chance I get.

Today I can be *peace in the chaos* or at least *kinda calm in the craziness*.

Today I can kiss a forehead, say "I am sorry. Please forgive me," and be the last one to let go in a hug.

Today I can sit beside my growing daughter and tell her what a remarkable baby she was and how much I love who she's becoming.

I am becoming too. Today matters more than yesterday.

Today I can bring peace to the breakfast table, to the morning good-bye, to the nighttime talks. These small acts of love act as bridges and bandages connecting us and healing past hurts.

Today is a good day. Today has hope yesterday doesn't have. And we are becoming.

Today's Reminder

Today is a brand-new chance to love and be loved. Even the briefest moment of loving connection holds the power to evoke healing and hope for the giver and the receiver. My goal is to get out of bed and greet myself and my family with love. Love is how I will start this day. Love is how I will end this day. May it transform all the minutes in between.

37

Introspection

Our stories are still being written, so
let's make them stories of love.

A Grand Possibility

Perhaps this month has been pretty rough so far.
Perhaps you're counting the days until the calendar flips to a new month, a new year, a new lease on life.
But wait. We can still salvage this long, hard month.
There is still time.
Our stories are still being written,
so let's make them stories of love,
of forgiveness,

of smiling-at-strangers kindness.
Let's make them stories of favorite recipes we haven't made in a while,
or re-reading that great book we adored the first time we read it.
Let's make our stories ones of morning snuggles and calling friends we haven't talked to in a while.
Let's make our stories about giving something away and holding something close.
Let's make our stories about loving words, empathy, and compassionate responses.
Let's make our stories shine with the resilience that is still alive in our weary hearts.
Let's make the remaining days of this month the shiniest part of a dark period.
Let's not wish away this period of our lives.
Let's see it for what it truly is: a grand possibility.
There is still time.
My friend, there is still time.

Today's Reminder

When I'm fighting my way back from a difficult place, it is helpful to focus on what I must see through. What must I do in this world that no one else can do? No matter how dismal things look right now, my story is still being written. I am not finished. I have a purpose in this world that only I can fulfill. I will let the hope and anticipation of an undiscovered goal fuel me forward today.

CONCLUSION: Looking Down

Love is the only thing required of you right now. And if love is the only thing you do today, that is enough. It is more than enough.

"Trouble finding us?" the receptionist asked quietly. Apparently my breathlessness and shaky hands gave me away.

Going anywhere unfamiliar has always been difficult for me. I'm what you'd call "directionally challenged." But I'd made a promise to myself, and that was to care for myself as I care for others. That promise gave me the motivation I needed to get past my fear of navigation and see yet another new doctor about one final and persistent, mysterious internal pain.

That morning, I'd equipped myself with two navigation systems and an extra forty-five-minute "cushion" to get to the appointment on time. I still managed to get lost. Once I finally found the office, located on the second floor of a large hospital, I got disoriented again. By the time I arrived, I was fifteen minutes late, sweaty, and out of breath.

Luckily, the receptionist was kind and said nothing about my tardiness. She gave me an understanding smile as she handed me a daunting stack of medical forms to fill out. I got through the first couple of lines okay, but when it came to my address, I could not remember my zip code. No matter how hard I tried to remember, the numbers escaped me.

"Got lost. Here now. Can't remember our zip," I texted my husband tearfully.

The five elusive numbers flashed back at me along with: "I'm sorry. Are you okay?"

That's when I looked down at my shaking hands. They'd filled out a lot of medical paperwork over the past twelve months. They'd been poked and prodded with many needles. They'd reached for a lot of unfamiliar hands donned in surgical gloves. But despite the ongoing struggle, these hands were still writing words to help others. They were still caring for the precious people in my home and extending kindness to those I encountered. These hands were faithfully implementing new self-care habits as I'd promised my older daughter. In other words, my hands were serving their most important purpose: to love.

Yes. Yes. As a matter of fact, I am okay, I thought to myself triumphantly. *I can see the dirt under my fingernails—the dirt that comes from holding on.*

My mind suddenly flashed back to the steep and curvy road leading to the entrance of my college. As a freshman I'd gotten myself in a bad situation. Late one night, the driver of the car I was in turned off the headlights and pressed on the gas, haphazardly hugging the road's narrow shoulder as he took each dangerous curve. Although I'd desperately wanted say, "Okay, man, that's enough," I could not speak. I was paralyzed in the backseat, gripping the door handle so tightly it felt like my fingernails were bleeding.

As the wind blew my hair back with a powerful force, it dawned on me that my window was open. That's the moment I began plotting, planning, and praying for my survival.

I decided that if the driver miscalculated a sharp turn and lost control, I would jump out the open window as the car tumbled into the ravine. I would then hang on to the edge of that steep incline with all my strength. I imagined myself being discovered at daybreak by my favorite English professor, who would be heading to her office to start her day. There I'd be, hanging on, my fingernails caked with dirt.

By the grace of God, I never had to implement that plan. I made it home safely that night, but the experience stuck with me indefinitely. During especially stressful and worrisome periods throughout my life, that dark, winding road resurfaces in my dreams. In fact, the night before each of my surgeries, I was back in that car. As the driver swerved this way and that way into pitch-black nothingness, I prayerfully recited my plan over and over: *Jump, then hang on. Dig your nails into the earth and don't let go. It is not your time to leave. You've got something important yet to do.*

As always, this recurring dream didn't have a happy (or tragic) ending—I woke up before it was over. But as usual, I felt comforted by it.

I could see the dirt under my nails.

I could see what was most important.

I could see what I had yet to do—and it was only one thing: *love. Just love.*

Love is the only thing required of me right now, I'd wake up thinking. *And if love is the only thing I do today, that is enough. It is more than enough.*

As I sat in that doctor's office, hands shaking, struggling to remember basic information, and facing more questions than answers, I felt an unexpected sense of peace. Yes, there were days when I would have preferred to avoid the pain, uncertainty, and hopelessness I'd repeatedly experienced over the past year, but the unresolved health issues had brought me here, to a place where God could reveal the dirt beneath my fingernails on a pair of hands being called to love. Just love. That is all. And now I can show you.

Take a moment and look down at your hands. See that dirt under your fingernails? My friend, that is beautiful. That is remarkable. That is significant.

You could have let go, but you didn't.

You could have given up, but you hung on.

You kept showing up, day after day, to love.

That is why I believe one small act of love holds transformative power.

When we choose love, we see, hear, taste, and smell beautiful things we would have missed.

When we choose love, we invite others to follow our lead.

When we choose love, joy is resuscitated inside our weary hearts.

When we choose love, angst diminishes and hope rises.

When we choose love, what matters in life becomes crystal clear.

In the presence of love, nothing else needs to be accomplished because no task is more important or more urgent than love. Ahhhh . . . doesn't that notion bring a big sigh of relief?

My friend, don't let the demanding voices in your head pressure you into thinking you must do more than you are called to do today. By using your favorite reminders in this book, you can hit the reset button and come back to *love . . . just love . . . only love.* You will do this many ways, but these are a few approaches we have touched on: by routinely checking the pressures building up inside you, by seeking and accepting the nourishments that quench your soul, by looking for the warm blankets in dismal situations, by reading and writing encouraging *notes to self* each day, by opening the window of your life and allowing healing light to pour in.

Although this is the end of the book, your story is far from over. There is something important you must do today and all the blessed days that follow. Simply look down at your hands and remember one word: *love.*

Love is the only thing required of you today.

Love is the only thing required of me today.

Together, with love, we'll breathe a sigh of relief and transform our world.

EPILOGUE

Only Love Today.

Use it as a mantra to shut down your inner bully that keeps you from loving this day, this you. Its critical and shaming tactics never motivated you anyway.

Only Love Today.

Use it as a reason to care for yourself—to get some exercise, drink more water, or make that long-overdue doctor's appointment. You are too important and too precious to be placed last on the priority list.

Only Love Today.

Use it as a three-second pause in moments of conflict. Three seconds gives you just enough time to see your loved ones as fallible human beings who count on you to love them, forgive them, and guide them. Three seconds is just enough time to "soften" so you can choose love.

Only Love Today.

Use it as a comeback to anyone being unkind or unfair to you. Use it as a proclamation to guard your time and energy. You have the right to set boundary lines and expectations of being treated with kindness, dignity, and respect.

Only Love Today.

Use it as a life motto, one you hope to pass down to those learning how to live by watching you live—not perfectly, but with small, positive steps and daily doses of grace.

Only Love Today.

Use it as a go-to phrase when you or someone you love makes a mistake that anyone who is human has made. Mistakes mean you are learning, trying, and growing.

Only Love Today.

Use it as a reminder that time is fleeting—why not fill it with the good stuff, the lasting stuff, the soul-building stuff? Life is too short to pass up extra hot fudge, spontaneous adventures, or a chance to smile at somebody.

Only Love Today.

Use it as a pledge to routinely turn away from what is negative and depleting and turn to what makes your heart feel hopeful and alive. Use it as perspective to notice there is goodness to be found within you and around you.

Only Love Today.

Use it as a prayer to grasp the glorious offerings of this day: a chance to love and be loved . . . a chance to live and let live . . . a time to celebrate . . . a time to breathe . . . a shot at peace . . . and one less regret tomorrow.

New York Times Bestseller!

Hands Free Mama

A Guide to Putting Down the Phone, Burning the To-Do List, and Letting Go of Perfection to Grasp What Really Matters!

Rachel Macy Stafford

> *"Rachel Macy Stafford's post "The Day I Stopped Saying Hurry Up" was a true phenomenon on The Huffington Post, igniting countless conversations online and off about freeing ourselves from the vicious cycle of keeping up with our overstuffed agendas. Hands Free Mama has the power to keep that conversation going and remind us that we must not let our lives pass us by."*
>
> —Arianna Huffington, Chair, President, and Editor-in-Chief of the Huffington Post Media Group, nationally syndicated columnist, and author of thirteen books http://www.huffingtonpost.com/

DISCOVER THE POWER, JOY, AND LOVE of Living "Hands Free"

In 2010, special education teacher and mother Rachel Macy Stafford decided enough was enough. Tired of losing track of what matters most in life, Rachel began practicing simple strategies that enabled her to let go of largely meaningless distractions and engage in meaningful soul-to-soul connections. She started a blog to chronicle her endeavors and soon saw how both external and internal distractions had been sabotaging her happiness and preventing her from bonding with the people she loves most.

Hands Free Mama is the digital society's answer to finding balance in a media-saturated, perfection-obsessed world. It doesn't mean giving up all technology forever. It doesn't mean forgoing our jobs and responsibilities. What it does mean is looking our loved ones in the eye and giving them the gift of our undivided attention, leaving the laundry till later to dance with our kids in the rain, and living a present, authentic, and intentional life despite a world full of distractions.

So join Rachel and go hands-free. Discover what happens when you choose to open your heart—and your hands—to each God-given moment.

Hands Free Life

Nine Habits for Overcoming Distraction, Living Better, and Loving More

Rachel Macy Stafford, New York Times Bestselling Author

We all yearn to look back to find we lived a life of significance. But is it even possible anymore? Considering the amount of distraction and pressure that exists in society today, living a fulfilling life may seem like an unachievable dream. But it is not--not with the nine habits outlined in this book.

New York Times bestselling author and widely known blogger, Rachel Macy Stafford, reveals nine habits that help you focus on investing in the most significant parts of your life. As your hands, heart, and eyes become open, you will experience a new sense of urgency--an urgency to live, love, dream, connect, create, forgive, and flourish despite the distractions of our culture.

By following each daily Hands Free Declaration, you will be inspired to adopt mindful daily practices and new thought-processes that will help you:

- Make meaningful, lasting human connections despite the busyness of everyday life.
- Live in the now despite that inner nudge pushing you out of the moment toward perfection and productivity.
- Protect your most sacred relationships, as well as your values, beliefs, health, and happiness, despite the latent dangers of technology and social media.
- Pursue the passions of your heart without sacrificing your job or your daily responsibilities.
- Evaluate your daily choices to insure you are investing in a life that matters to you.

With a Hands Free Life perspective, you will have the power to look back and see you didn't just manage life, you actually lived it--and lived it well.